# 50 EVENING ADVENTURES

## TIM, KERRY, AMY AND ELLA MEEK

FRANCES
LINCOLN

# 50 EVENING ADVENTURES

## TIM, KERRY, AMY AND ELLA MEEK

**To our family and friends**

Frances Lincoln Limited
74-77 White Lion Street
London N1 9PF

*50 Evening Adventures* by Tim, Kerry, Amy and Ella Meek
Copyright © Frances Lincoln Limited 2016
Text ©The Meek Family 2016
Photographs © The Meek Family, except where listed on page 128

First Frances Lincoln edition 2016

A catalogue record for this book is available from the British Library.

978-0-7112-3755-1

9 8 7 6 5 4 3 2 1

Printed in China

Quarto is the authority on a wide range of topics.

Quarto educates, entertains and enriches the lives of
our readers – enthusiasts and lovers of hands-on living.

www.QuartoKnows.com

# CONTENTS

# INTRODUCTION

Do any of the following sound familiar:?

- Is work consuming your life and eating into your family time?
- Do you sometimes feel like you are living only for the weekends?
- Are you stuck for ideas about what to do when you eventually get to spend time with the kids?
- Do you want your children to spend less time on computer screens and in front of the TV?
- Do you feel as if you're never 'off duty' but always 'on call' for work 24/7?

If you have answered 'Yes' to any of these, you're not alone. Many parents are also struggling with how to manage a busy work life alongside the demands of family life and spending quality time with their children. By quality time we mean screen-free, outdoor time, full of interaction, fun and activity. Our fast-paced modern 21st-century lifestyle and a culture that promotes long working hours often means that time with loved ones gets crowded out or, at best, relegated to the bottom of a long 'to do' pile.

Well, it's time to do something about it. 50 Evening Adventures is designed to help you achieve a more rewarding outdoor and adventure-filled lifestyle that is less orientated around work and more family focused. We've written this book to help you adjust your work-life balance and inject some quality family time back into your life – not only at the weekends, but also during the working week, between the hours of clocking off from work and the time the kids go to bed. These weekday periods from 5-9(pm) offer the perfect opportunity to squeeze in some bite-sized evening adventures.

You might be asking yourself 'How can I manage that if I'm so busy all the time?' It's a fair point, but hopefully this book will show you that with a little bit of preparation, some ideas of **what** to do and some advice on **how** to do it, anyone can find time to enhance their lives with a bit of excitement, a sense of reward and even a spot of adventure too.

Living for the weekends is often a default response, a survival mechanism for those caught up in a work-heavy lifestyle. While this may offer a temporary respite and a chance to 'come up for air' and reclaim some much-needed family time, more often the weekend arrives and, what with the rush of the week before, little thought or preparation has gone into planning any structure or activities for the two-day break. Before you know it, the weekend has come and gone in a blink of an eye, Monday is here again, the manic schedule resumes and the weekend has been wasted.

Clichés about children growing up fast can take on an unnerving reality: 'they grow so quickly', 'blink and you'll miss them', 'before you know it they are gone'. Wishing time away can sometimes bring with it an emotional guilt about missed story times and wasted opportunities for spending time together. Indeed the very notion of living for the weekends means you are 'writing off' five days out of every seven. *50 Evening Adventures* allows you to take stock and begin to create a pro-active and creative approach to family time management.

Clocking off and staying disconnected from email and mobile devices is just as important for adults as it is children. Don't allow yourself to be on call 24/7. Allocate a minimum amount of time for winding down and eating (or preparing some food to take with you) then try to spend a night or two being active outside the house. You'll be surprised how energising it can be, even if you arrived home shattered and stressed from a hard day at the office. Instead of going for a

solo run, think about some active exercise with which the whole family can join in. Start to think about the 5-9pm part of the day as much as you do the 9-5. Here are some of the fun family adventures and ideas in the book:

- Suggestions of places to GO, from harbours and marinas to gardens and allotments and how to make the most of them.
- Plenty of ideas for things to DO (make, build, investigate, climb, hide, paddle, cycle, explore, create...)
- A selection of recipes and cooking advice for a range of family-favourite meals that can be cooked outdoors with the minimum of equipment to allow you to 'eat out' in style together and make the most of your time outdoors.
- Sensible guidance on health and safety considerations to help you keep you and your children safe and happy.
- An abundance of tips and advice for getting the most out of your midweek evening adventures.

If you like the sound of this, and you're already excited about the prospect of clocking off and living less for work and more for family time – or you just simply need some ideas and inspiration – then read on and start preparing for your first weekday evening adventure.

## HAVE FUN!

GO...

# GO BEACH/CLIFF

**A beach is synonymous with fun and excitement, and a blast of sea air is the perfect tonic after a hard day at school or at work.**

Whether you can get to a beach easily or not depends on where you live; let's face it, if your home is not near the sea, getting to a beach of an evening is going to be a little bit difficult. But for those that do live near a coast, there are no excuses for not hitting the sand, except perhaps for a high tide!

Beaches are great places in which to spend time with kids. There are plenty of opportunities for children to play creatively in a large space with a degree of freedom, while at the same time staying safe. These are sensory-rich places: feel the sand between your toes, the acoustic rhythms of the sea and the breeze kissing your face. Cliffs, meanwhile, offer the opportunity to go on a fossil hunt below them and enjoy the great views from the top of them.

In short, beaches and cliffs can give kids the wild release they require – just spending 15 minutes on a beach at the end of the day will make a child feel happy, and smiley inside.

## HEALTH & SAFETY
- Be aware of tide times, particularly high tide.
- Cliffs can be dangerous, so take care when on or below them.
- Make sure children are always supervised around water.

## TIPS FOR HAVING FUN

- Visit a beach during the late afternoon or early evening – they are much quieter then.
- Take some binoculars and look out for birds and sea life, or distant ships.
- Take a bucket to collect things in, but always make sure you put living things back where they came from.
- Pick up some litter and leave the beach cleaner than when you arrived.

### AMY SAYS:

The best fossil I've ever found was a large ammonite and it was just lying on the beach! Why don't you try making a fossil collection – there are loads of different ones to find!

# GO BIKE AND SKATE PARK

**Places for excitement and thrills, for stunts and tricks, or just a moment to cruise, roll and chillax.**

Most cities and towns have a 'park' of some sort where kids can go to skate, board or bike. They can be places brimming with raw talent and riders passionate to learn new skills and express themselves.

There is also, usually, a culture of mutual support and respect that acknowledges achievement, and ignores and even accepts failure as par for the course; if you don't fall, you're not pushing yourself.

If your child is young and/or a beginner, go when it is fairly quiet – that way, you can ride or skate without getting in anyone's way. And then when it starts to get busier, take a seat on the peripheries and watch and learn from the more experienced users.

**HEALTH & SAFETY**
- Always wear a helmet when skating /biking /scootering.
- Take care when it's damp or wet – your wheels need plenty of friction!

## TIPS FOR HAVING FUN

- Go in the early evening, when the younger kids are out – there's less of a chance of meeting any unruly types.
- Start small and gradually extend your skills and confidence. Don't be tempted to do anything to look cool – the chances are it will end in a fall.
- In the winter months – with their shorter nights – skate or ride with a head torch for extra fun and excitement.
- Film some short video clips of the action and make a short action sports film when you get home.

### AMY SAYS:

I like watching the locals and trying to learn some of their tricks. Here are some trick names: tail whip, ollie, bunny hop, manual.

# GO  CITY/TOWN/VILLAGE CENTRE

**See what's happening at the heart of where you live.**

Traditionally 'centres' of places were where everything happened; they were the heartbeat of a place. The 'hub of the hubbub' if you like. This might or might not be the case today – so go and find out.

It's likely that activity will vary depending on the time of year and the time of day: a city centre might be converted into a pop-up beach in the summer holidays or a Christmas Market in December; a village green might host a travelling fairground at times throughout the year and the local cricket team in the drier months. In the hours after work and school, these places change in character too; as the buskers pack up and head home, skateboarders or parkour runners may well replace them.

Your local 'centre' will open up opportunities to watch, explore, get active, get involved and get adventurous if you take the time to get to know it.

### HEALTH & SAFETY
- After hours, centres and hubs of cities, towns or villages can be busy places, so road safety awareness definitely applies, especially to children.
- Cities and towns can have unruly elements, particularly at weekends.
- As ever, wear helmets if scootering, cycling or skateboarding.

### TIPS FOR HAVING FUN
- Compare and contrast the same 'centre' by visiting at different times of the year.
- Take a picnic or meal to cook and eat 'out' instead of sitting in a stuffy pub or restaurant.
- Sit and observe the 'goings on' for a while – people (and the things they do) are often fascinating.
- Be creative and come up with some mini-adventure ideas: climb the equivalent of a mountain by walking up stairs and steps in the city centre; take a sledge in winter and look for places to slide; set-up a slackline in a green space that has a dramatic background; go on a night walk (or a ghost hunt if you are brave).

### ELLA SAYS:
There are often markets in the centre of cities, towns and villages with a range of food and craft stalls. I like looking at, and smelling, the food on sale and asking about the local delicacies.

# GO  FOREST/WOOD

Kids find forests and wooded areas naturally exciting places to spend time, so give them some space and let them enjoy the freedom.

Regardless of the time of year, woods and forests are worth a visit. In fact, it's worth making a conscious decision to visit during different seasons to see how the flora and fauna change throughout the year and to explore the different seasonal opportunities for mini-adventuring.

You can go with a specific focus – such as to watch wildlife, ride or run, collect, make or build something, or simply to have a walk and enjoy quality fresh-air time together.

Visits to a wood or forest will lead you to become more familiar with your native species of trees, flowers and birds, and that's something rewarding, particularly for children. It shows a true connection with nature, and that can only be a good thing.

**HEALTH & SAFETY**
- Woods and forests often have spiky, sticky-out bits that can scratch and puncture – make little ones aware of them.
- Watch out during 'fungi season' that children don't mess with potentially dangerous mushrooms or toadstools – that wouldn't be much fun at all.

## TIPS FOR HAVING FUN

- Take your bikes along – forests are great places in which to ride.
- Expect to get muddy – both adults and kids. In fact, tell the kids not to worry about getting dirty. Too often getting muddied-up is frowned upon… it's not as if mud is a dirty word!
- Take a small handsaw and a knife with you for some spontaneous whittling.
- Go off the beaten track and make up your own route.
- Make a hideout just off the path and see if anyone spots you.
- Take a torch and go for a walk in the dark – trees look very different at night.

### AMY SAYS:

I remember when we went to a forest at night and there were bats everywhere. Our dad was throwing up small stones and they swooped low over our heads, momentarily mistaking them for insects.

# GO GARDEN AND ALLOTMENT

**Get into the right frame of mind, and you'll find there's a lot of fun activities you can do in your garden or allotment.**

If you are lucky enough to have a garden, ask yourself a question, 'do you make the most of it, all year round?' If the answer is no, then hopefully this page will help you to do so.

One of the ways to get more out of your garden is to try and make it more suitable for outdoor play and activity all year round, by designating an area for artificial grass. This could be around a swing or slide, or in an open area for ball games. Artificial grass may not be everybody's favourite, but it will banish muddy footprints in the house during winter – a 'win win' for kids and parents!

An allotment or vegetable patch can also be a source of 'edventure' all year round, as there will always be lots to do and find out about.

**HEALTH & SAFETY**
- If you put decking down as a play surface, paint some anti-slip strips on it to prevent falls.
- Make sure little ones know how to use garden tools safely, and always supervise them.

## TIPS FOR HAVING FUN

- Dedicate an area of the garden or allotment to the kids, and let them decide what they want to use it for. If the kids have ownership of the garden, they'll use it more.
- For an exciting and interesting garden, make it wildlife-friendly: leave food out for hedgehogs and foxes; leave gaps at the bottom of fences so animals can get in/out; make a range of shelters for frogs and mini-beasts.
- Go out in all weathers, throughout the year. There's no such thing as bad weather, just the wrong clothing i.e. wrap up warm and keep dry, and don't allow some wet weather to keep you out of your garden.

### AMY SAYS:

I enjoy picking the apples from our apple tree in the autumn and then munching on them for the next few days! Freshly picked fruit always seems to taste better than shop-bought stuff.

# GO HARBOUR/MARINA/PIER

A visit to the coast to see fishermen, boats, and maybe even rides and amusements, is sure to provide a midweek highlight.

Coastal villages and towns are steeped in history, so go on a hunt for clues about ancient smuggling, or stories about a place's maritime past. If the fishing trade is still in operation, learn about it by speaking to the locals and watching the activity around the harbour.

Marinas are fascinating places to explore and are often hosts to vessels visiting from overseas. The boats vary from small day cruisers to large yachts and powerboats. Often there is some indication of their home/ destination in their names or the flags they fly.

Piers stretch out precariously into the sea, vulnerable to the daily beatings of the ocean and the corrosion of salt water. As a result, they often have dramatic stories associated with them that coincide with infamous storms and severe weather events. But of course it's the attractions they house that are likely to be the highlight of any child's visit.

## HEALTH & SAFETY
- Keep an eye on inquisitive young ones around the edges of piers, jetties and sea walls.
- Gulls can be aggressive around children holding food.
- If sea birds are flying overhead, don't look up – you might get an eyeful.

## TIPS FOR HAVING FUN

- Get as high up as you can (walk up the nearest cliff path) and look down on the harbour or marina – it gives you a fresh perspective and a 'bigger picture' view of the activities and movements.
- Head down to see a harbour when the weather is cold, windy and rainy, and the sea is rough and angry – it will make you appreciate how tough life is for fishermen.
- Take your crabbing line and some bits of old bacon and try to catch the crabs that come out around the base of the harbour as the tide comes in.
- Go for a run, scooter or cycle ride along the sea front and pier (if there is one) and enjoy a blast of sea air.

### AMY SAYS:

Try to find a fishing boat that has just come in and watch the catch being sorted. Also, go on a trail around the harbour – try and spot at least three bits of fishing equipment.

# GO HILLS AND MOUNTAINS

Hill? Mountain? Who cares which? Wander or saunter, run or climb as high above sea level as you can get.

If you live close enough to a mountain to be able to ascend it one evening after work/school, then lucky you! You have the perfect location for a midweek adventure in the outdoors. If you don't have a mountain on your doorstep, then look for the highest hill in your locality. Failing that, look for a hillock!

Getting into the hills or mountains is one of the best ways to wind down from the stresses of work and school (kids get stressed too, you know). The views are good for the spirit and the strenuous act of hauling yourself up there in the first place gets the heart and lungs working healthily. Pack a rucksack with a few essential basics (map, binoculars and refreshments) so you can admire the view, watch the sun set and have a well-deserved snack at the top – the perfect evening adventure.

## HEALTH & SAFETY

- If going into the mountains, the usual hill walking safety applies (see page 124).
- Wear appropriate clothing for the walk, and make sure the little ones know not to run downhill… EVER.

## TIPS FOR HAVING FUN

- Start small, then work your way up to climbing up bigger and bigger hills or mountains. Once you start to build up your stamina, you'll be surprised what you can manage in a single evening.
- For young walkers it's important to make sure they enjoy the experience – otherwise they won't want to do it again. So make sure you have plenty of time to complete the walk, including time to stop, munch, drink, look and smile.
- Join a local walking group and make your evening climb a social event. If there isn't a local group, start one yourself by encouraging other family adventurers to join you.

## ELLA SAYS:

It's fascinating to know how mountains form. Plates of earth push up against each other and force the land up. Look out for the lines in the rock that might still be there from when a mountain was formed.

# GO CASTLE/HISTORIC BUILDING

Travel back in time for an evening adventure at a historic location and relive the past.

The chances are that many historic buildings might close their doors in the early evening, or earlier in the winter months, but this shouldn't deter you from making a visit 'after hours' as you are still likely to be able to wander around the grounds. In doing so, you'll see the place in a different light – literally – and experience the change in atmosphere that comes with a dark, stormy evening when the building might look ominous, or a warm summer's evening when it is bathed in 'golden-hour' sunshine. As there are  fewer people around, this adds to the sense of atmosphere and adventure.

**HEALTH & SAFETY**
- If you enter gated grounds towards the end of the day, be aware of closing times to prevent you and your car from being locked in.
- Don't try and climb any walls or fences to gain access if the place is locked.

## TIPS FOR HAVING FUN

- Take your camera and try to get some arty photos or take video footage so you can make a short film that captures the atmosphere during your visit.
- The grounds of many castles and historic buildings come alive with nightlife – in the form of animals, not party-goers – so if you are quiet and watchful you might get close to deer, rabbits and foxes. You can be sure that even if you are not watching them, they will be watching you!
- If there is a story attached to the building, take it along and find somewhere in the grounds or ruins to sit and read the story together. Take a ghost story along only if you are feeling very brave!

## AMY SAYS:

Ok, historic buildings can be a little boring, so use your imagination! This may be a little hard if the building is in ruins, but try to picture it in its prime, swarming with inhabitants and possibly being attacked from the outside – starting to sound a little more fun?

# GO LAKE/LOCH

You can bank on a lake or loch to provide opportunities for fun and adventure, if not a view of a loch monster!

Natural bodies of water like lakes and lochs vary hugely in size and use (so too do their access arrangements). Some will have lakeside walks or trails, while others may offer watersports activities or have wildlife hides you can use to spy on the resident wildlife. Some may be off-limits completely due to their usage or because they have steep banks and are therefore dangerous. Make sure you familiarize yourself with the lake that you propose to visit.

Some lakes have wild swimming groups associated with them that offer sessions for beginners. This is the best way to give the growing pastime of wild swimming a try. Similarly, local wildlife groups might meet in the evenings and offer guided wildlife walks around the area for families to join in on.

**HEALTH & SAFETY**
- Look out for signs warning of blue-green algae in the water – it can be toxic for children and dogs.
- Make sure children wear buoyancy aids when at the water's edge or out on the water.
- Take care near steep banks.

## TIPS FOR HAVING FUN

- Get some local knowledge about when you are most likely to see visiting birds using the lake as a temporary stop-off during a migratory journey.
- Pack your binoculars and a wildlife guide.
- Take your swimwear and a towel in case there's a chance of a wild swim or a paddle to cool the feet down.
- See if you can walk the perimeter of the lake. When you get home, measure the distance on Google maps to see how far you travelled.

## ELLA SAYS:

I learned to sail at a local lake and spent many weekends splashing around with sailing buddies. There was a small island in the middle that we used to sail to and have hot chocolate – yum yum!

#  NATURE RESERVE/MEADOW

Watch, listen, and enjoy being at one with nature.

The natural world is all around us – in fields, meadows and reserves – and while we may kid ourselves that we notice nature, we probably don't actually 'see it'. Yet the ability to observe, enjoy and tune into nature is available to us all; we simply have to take the time to do it.

An evening expedition (OK, a walk) to a local meadow or a nature reserve, combined with the act of sitting quietly, looking and listening, will return huge rewards. The longer you sit, the more you notice. In fact, you'll probably find that your senses become overloaded with scents from flowers and grasses, noises of nearby insects busying themselves around you, more distant sounds of birds taking to the roost for the night, and the textures and temperatures of the natural world you touch.

Learn to fully appreciate the natural world, and help your youngsters do the same.

**HEALTH & SAFETY**
- Be aware of any allergies a child may have that are triggered by any specific plants or insect bites/stings and take the necessary medications.

## TIPS FOR HAVING FUN

- Look with your eyes closed. This sounds a bit odd, but we often become too reliant on the sense of sight, so it's an interesting exercise to sit down and close or cover the eyes for a few minutes and just listen. It takes a bit of getting used to, but with practice you will learn to 'see' a new version of the world.
- Wildlife-related activities and visits are always much more rewarding when you can identify (with confidence) what it is you are seeing – so take a guidebook. If ever you are in doubt, take a photo, sketch or audio recording and find out what it is when you get back home.
- Invite a friend along and share the knowledge you have with them – they then might do the same with someone else.

### ELLA SAYS:

I love animals, so I enjoy going to nature reserves to watch them. Talking to the experts and finding out about the animals there is always an interesting thing to do.

# GO OUTDOOR SPACE

**Go outdoors, find a space – Yay! it's so simple to source an outdoor space to enjoy together.**

Everyone has an outdoor space close by to enjoy after hours – it could be a playground, recreation field or an outdoor gym – it doesn't really matter where it is. Ideally it will have some natural flora; you know, something green with leaves growing from the ground. It's a bonus if there's some fauna there too. The simple act of going somewhere that has plants and wildlife will make you feel better – and your kids will feel better too. Also, when in such a space, there's more chance that you will do something active – running around, playing tag, working out on the gym, shooting baskets or playing football-based games like Headers and Volleys. Being active and exercising will get your 'feel-good' endorphins flowing for an increased sense of well-being.

We all have these spaces and options available to us; it's a matter of whether we choose to enjoy them or not.

**HEALTH & SAFETY**
- Gym equipment is usually built for adults or large children, so supervise small children to ensure they don't hurt themselves.
- Take a few minutes before you start to check your play area is free of dog mess (and any other potentially harmful objects).

## TIPS FOR HAVING FUN

- Arrange to head down to the local park or outdoor space with other families – team games are much more fun if there are plenty of participants.
- Have a 'play-gear bag' constantly packed full of balls, bats, rackets, marker cones and any other outdoor play equipment you may have, and take it along whenever you head out to an open space.
- Take some refreshments: drinks, fruit, ice pops and have scheduled 'time outs' when everyone can take on energy and liquid... as well as just chat.
- Playgrounds can sometimes attract an unruly element, particularly after dark, so get there early to miss them.

## ELLA SAYS:

I love playing imaginative games, energetic games and team games with other children. One of my favourites is Capture the Flag. I also like to play Dobby Off Ground at the park.

# GO  PUBLIC ART

## Enjoy discovering public art in your local area.

Public art refers to any piece of art (and remember art can refer to a range of different interpretations) that is created and exhibited with the intention of it being freely accessible to the general public.

Apart from the obvious types of art you'll probably already be familiar with, such as statues and sculptures, you might be surprised by the other kinds of art you might find in your local area once you actively look for it. If you're not sure what's available, contact the local council as they will have a list of all public art. As you explore your area, look out for installations such as outdoor paintings, murals and montages, mazes and artwork that explore the use of light (best visited at night-time, of course). Some cities and larger towns might have an active urban art community that creates street art (which is different to graffiti-tagging) to explore and enjoy.

### HEALTH & SAFETY
- Avoid areas littered with graffiti-tagging (ugly 'signatures' sprayed to mark territory) as these might not be desirable places to be, especially at night.

## TIPS FOR HAVING FUN

- As you explore your area, mark any artistic 'finds' on a map (one you've made yourself is better than a bought one). Show your map to friends, spread the word and share the art.
- Make sketches of any street art that you like the look of, and make up your own designs. Take photographs that you can refer to when you get home and do some follow-up designing.
- Look out for an organized street-art tour to join. If there isn't one, start your own by finding out about the history of the art and the stories behind their creation.

### ELLA SAYS:

I like learning about the history associated with statues, but also find them very entertaining when there are birds sitting on them!

# GO RIVER/STREAM/CANAL

**Being around water is good for the mind and soul; it is both relaxing and exhilarating. It also captivates the enquiring minds of youngsters and can spark their imagination.**

Whether you live in a rural or an urban area, there is likely to be a body of inland water of some description within a relatively short distance from where you live. Take a look at a local map and you'll quickly identify your local water source. Different water types offer different experiences:

**RIVERS** often have bank paths to walk along that let you get close to the water's edge, particularly if there is a river beach to access. They also often carry a shocking amount of litter and rubbish that people have dropped or thrown in.

**CANALS** have paths you can walk or even ride along they and they are also very flat – perfect for wheelchair users too.

**STREAMS** often have steep banks leading to them and can be fast-flowing; harder to access, but great for paddling, dam-building and general exploring.

**HEALTH & SAFETY**
- Supervise young children carefully at all times when around water.
- Watch out for slippery banks along the edges of rivers and streams.
- Take extra care around canal locks.

## TIPS FOR HAVING FUN

- If the kids are planning on getting wet, dress them in their 'wet gear' before you set off — it's easier and faster to get changed into a wetsuit at home than at the water's edge. But don't forget to take a towel and clothes to change back into.
- When visiting a river, take a bin bag and litter picker (and gloves) so that you can leave the river and its banks cleaner than you found them.
- A quiet and stealthy wildlife river walk is likely to result in rewarding views of river life. Dress in natural colours, take some binoculars and a wildlife book and keep your eyes peeled.
- Offer to help at canal locks; manual lock gates can be difficult to push, so the more people pushing, the better.

### AMY SAYS:

Take your wetsuit along on your visit to the river and a rubber ring. Rivers with some rapids make great courses for tubing but make sure you have an exit point nearby. Bring it on!

# GO STREET

Reinstate childhood down your street – even if just for one night, or get to know your local area like you've never known it before.

If you don't have time in the evening to go very far (shorter winter days, access to a car isn't an option or rush-hour traffic made you late home) then stay local and look literally down your own street for something to do and ways to maximize the time between the end of school/work and bedtime story-hour for the kids.

Once upon a time, the local streets and cul-de-sacs were where kids used to hang out after school: playing ball games, riding bikes and generally being kids. Try to reinstate this childhood entitlement down your street if you can – even for just one evening. Get other parents involved to make the street safe for the kids to just 'play out'. The sad irony is that should you manage this, the kids will feel like they've experienced something new and exciting.

Alternatively, get on your bike, scooter or skateboard and explore your local area to experience 'instant' history, to see what people get up to or where they go in the evening. It's a big world out there, but your street is the perfect place to start experiencing it!

**HEALTH & SAFETY**
- Make sure kids are aware of any dangers that might exist in their neighbourhood – road safety, stranger danger etc.
- Ensure kids wear helmets when cycling and scootering around.

## TIPS FOR HAVING FUN

- Do something in your locality that helps you see it in a new way: find out where a local club meets (bowls, tennis or a photography club for instance) and watch or join in with them.
- Learn some road names and new routes. Look out for anyone looking lost and help them with navigating to where they are hoping to go.
- Get as many people involved in a street reclaim as possible – safety and powers in numbers, and all that.
- Make some 'Children Playing' or 'Kill Your Speed' signs and posters to put up in the local area to help calm traffic speeds.

## ELLA SAYS:

I like people watching and imagining where they have come from and where they might be going. It's fun to make up weird and wonderful stories about them.

# GO   VIEWPOINT

**The kind of viewpoint you find can actually depend on your own point of view.**

A viewpoint, also otherwise known as a vista or scenic overlook, generally implies getting on to a high vantage point and enjoying a view of some kind. You often see viewpoint opportunities on mountain or hill roads, on corners or 'pull-offs' or lay-bys (pull-ins) – places where you can take a welcome rest from pedalling and catch a view as you catch your breath.

Of course, your viewpoint can be something much smaller, more local, more immediate: the top of a rise in a forest, the top of a monument mound in a town or city, a vista from a crag or escarpment. What you decide to be your viewpoint depends on your point of view of what one is. And that's the point; there are no right or wrongs. It's more about the defining then finding the viewpoint that is important... not how grand or well known it is to other people.

## HEALTH & SAFETY
- It's stating the obvious, but hilly roads with lots of corners and long drops are an occupational hazard when getting to and from the bigger mountain/hill viewpoints.
- Isolated viewpoints offer quietness and tranquillity as well as great views, but take a map and compass to ensure you don't get lost.

## TIPS FOR HAVING FUN

- Look for a west-facing viewpoint to visit and get there in time for a sunset.
- Don't forget to look at your map when you reach the viewpoint; it can really help you spot landmarks and features in the distance.
- Take a tripod or make one out of sticks/walking sticks to ensure you get that perfect selfie of all participants, with your viewpoint in the background.
- Remember your binoculars and camera — for obvious reasons — as you'll be gutted if you get to your vista without them.

## AMY SAYS:

It can be a struggle getting to a viewpoint, but it is definitely worth it when you reach the point, for an obvious reason! I recommend visiting one when the sun is setting or rising — I like watching the area around become bathed in golden light as it's very beautiful.

DO...

# DO   BUILD SOMETHING

Kids love to build things, particularly if it means getting hands-on and dirty outdoors. Making a structure with your kids while collaborating on a shared goal can help to build positive family relationships.

In order to build something you will need to source some raw materials. The materials you need depend on what it is you want to build, of course and, to a large extent, what you can build will vary according to your location – it's going to be pretty tricky building a sand castle if you are not near a beach for instance. So, choose your project carefully to ensure you can make the most of materials that are close to hand. Also check that you can start and finish the job in the time you have available. Completing the build is not the be-all and end-all, as the process is important too, but a finished project is certainly very rewarding.

### BUILD... A HIBERNATION STATION
Animals such as hedgehogs need a cosy and protected place in which to sleep during the colder months. Just by building a pile of twigs and branches you could be helping this spiny species to survive (hedgehogs are in decline in the UK). And while you are at it, gather some branches and twigs (and grasses) with hollow stems and nestle them between some bigger logs or stones and – voila! – you'll have made a bug hotel for the smaller bugs and critters (otherwise known as mini-beasts). Two good deeds in one – job done.

### BEAT THE CLOCK
Do some forward planning the night before and gather together specific equipment (like a saw, a fire-starter or tarpaulin etc.) and clothing (like gloves, rain boots or buckets etc.).

## BUILD... A WILDLIFE HIDE

Ensure a close-up view of wildlife by making a simple hide using natural materials. Push some sticks into the ground to act as fence posts. Next, interweave thin branches and twigs through them to form a rough fence. Pile grass and leaves on top to make it super-camouflaged, then position yourselves behind it and 'hide'.

**TIP** Leave a viewing hole to peek through and stay very still and quiet. Keep a record of anything you spot.

## BUILD... A DAM

Dams can be constructed in streams, in shallow sections of rivers or at the beach. All they require you to do is to trap or block some flowing water. When you've had enough of building your epic mega-structure, throw stones at its walls in an attempt to cause a breach. See how strong it is and how long it holds. You could even sing: 'Who ya gonna call? Dambusters!'

# DO BURY SOMETHING

**Don't bury your head in the sand. Try using your feet – or something else instead!**

Squirrels bury nuts, dogs bury bones and ostriches bury their heads! Us humans also like to bury a wide range of items for different reasons. Choose a burying activity according to the location that you are going to and the interests of the family. Historians may enjoy creating a time capsule that will inform the future about our contemporary world, whereas nature-lovers might like to get their hands dirty in the garden. And surely everyone will join in burying mum or dad in the sand!

Here are some burying ideas:

### BURY … SEEDS OR BULBS

Potatoes are one of the treasures of the gardening world; it's exciting to try to find perfect potatoes growing among the roots underground. But in order to reap the rewards, you need to do some digging in the garden or allotment. Choose which vegetables or flowers you want to grow and follow the instructions on the packet. Then wait patiently for the results.

### BURY… A TIME CAPSULE

A time capsule is a miniature archive of objects that represents the current period in which we live. The capsule is buried in the hope that future historians will find it and get a snapshot of what life was like for us.

To make your own time capsule, you need a waterproof/weatherproof container in which to put your chosen items. Don't forget to stick on a label or add a note explaining what year it is. The location is quite important because you don't want it to be found easily in the near future, so choose wisely.

### BEAT THE CLOCK

This activity will involve some planning, discussion and possibly some research. Think carefully about what you want to put in the capsule and prepare the contents before you GO to your location and DO this activity.

## BURY... TREASURE

Pretend to be a pirate and bury some treasure in the woods or on the beach. To help you or someone else find it, create a map with an **X** to mark the spot where the treasure is hidden. You could give the map to fellow pirates or return to the spot another day to see if your treasure is still there.

## BURY... FEET

Kids always love to bury feet in the sand, either their own or someone else's. It's fun to stand at the water's edge and let your feet sink and squidge into wet sand or, better still, to bury a volunteer's feet as they soak up the rays. But you don't need to stop there; you could bury them up to their neck! Just watch out for sand fleas.

# DO   CAST SOMETHING

**Get creative with plaster of Paris and see your ideas set in stone forever.**

Plaster of Paris (gypsum plaster) is a powdery material that can be bought from craft shops, online or even DIY or hardware stores and is easy to use. It sets quite quickly, making it an ideal substance to use with children to make models and casts.

## Mixing plaster of Paris

- A guide for the ratio of plaster powder to water is 1:2 (that's one part water to two parts plaster powder).

- Take a bowl and add 'one part' of water. Gradually sprinkle the 'two parts' of plaster powder into the water (don't stir yet).

- Tap the side of the bowl to remove any powder stuck to the sides of the bowl and release air bubbles.

- Stir slowly so as not to create air bubbles.

- Leave the mixture to stand for a minute.

- Pour into your mould.

**N.B.** Plaster of Paris can be an irritant, so make sure it doesn't come into contact with the skin or eyes. Take care not to inhale the powdery dust and make sure children are supervised.

### CAST... PET PRINTS
Capture your pet's paw print in damp sand, mud or a Plasticine (modelling clay) cast.

### CAST... ANIMAL PRINTS
Track and cast a wild animal such as a deer or rabbit – or a grisly bear. Or make fake prints of dinosaurs or mythical monsters such as the Yeti!

### CAST... FAMILY PRINTS
Capture the footprint or handprint of a brother or sister and then make a cast. Parents are soppy about this kind of thing. Scratch the name and date in the plaster before it dries –you might even be able to sell the cast.

### CAST ... A TOY PRINT
Make a Plasticine (modelling clay) mould of a favourite Lego figure or toy soldier etc. then make plaster models to paint.

Paint your casts once they've dried and varnish them using **PVA** glue. The glue is see-through when it dries, so it will make your models look smart and shiny.

### BEAT THE CLOCK
To save scrambling around looking for plaster of Paris at the last minute (and to avoid any disappointment) order some online well in advance of when you are intending to use it.

# DO  CLEAN UP SOMETHING

Litter not only looks ugly, but also it can be devastating for wildlife and even inflict suffering on animals and birds, so do your bit to clean up a local area.

This activity will leave you with a warm, feel-good sensation, the kind that you only get after you've done a good deed, a gesture of kindness or goodwill that helps someone, or something.

There are likely to be lots of places in your local area that could do with a bit of a clean-up, so this activity is a good one to use as a time-filler for when you want to have a midweek adventure that doesn't take too much planning or preparation.

### CLEAN UP WITH...  A LITTER PICK
Organise a 5-minute clean-up. Many hands make light work and the impact on the environment can be significant. A session of group litter-picking spreads awareness and encourages people to be more litter-aware.

Choose a local area that you can visit and clean regularly. You'll see it gradually become cleaner over the weeks and feel a real sense of achievement and pride.

Prevention is better than cure. Make a poster to spread awareness or think of how to spread the word via social media.

### CLEAN UP WITH...  A LITTER SPEAR
Sharpen a stick with a knife (under parental supervision) and use it as a homemade litter picker-upper.

### CLEAN UP WITH...  A STATEMENT
Make a statement out of rubbish that you have found. You could perhaps spell the words 'Pick it up' or 'Bin it'.

### BEAT THE CLOCK
Have your litter-cleaning kit (picker-upper, gloves and bags) ready by the back door or in the boot of the car.

# DO CLIMB SOMETHING

What goes up must come down... and then probably goes up again, particularly if we are talking about children and climbing. Many children love to climb, so tap into this fun activity for a spot of adventure.

Climbing is about using your hands, feet, knees, fingers, toes, elbows... in fact any body part (within reason), to ascend something or travel along something (known as traversing). What you decide to climb defines what sort of climber you are: a tree climber, a rock climber or a climbing-frame climber.

Playgrounds are good spaces in which to hone climbing skills, particularly traversing, as well as improve balance, strength and flexibility. All of these key skills can, and should be well developed before venturing too hight off the ground.

All climbing is exciting and thrilling to try (except perhaps 'social' climbing – give that one a miss) so have fun, but stay within your ability.

**Tip** Soft, close-fitting shoes are best for climbing because they allow you to gain good friction against the wall, rock or tree.

### BEAT THE CLOCK
Get to know the playgrounds, woods and parks in your area so that when you decide to set out to climb, you can head to the best spots.

### CLIMB... A TREE
This is a classic activity that is talked about often these days by the older generation when they reminisce.

Make sure that the kids can identify suitable trees to climb as follows:
**TYPE** Oak, ash or beech.
**CONDITION** A strong and healthy tree; no rotting branches. Firm, strong branches (at least as thick as your arm) at regular intervals.
**TECHNIQUE** Climb close to the trunk and test each branch before you trust it with your full body weight. Face the trunk as you climb down the tree and use your legs to find footholds.

### CLIMB... YOUR SELF-NAMED ROUTE
In the climbing world, if you complete a route no-one else has, you can name it, e.g. Hilary's Step on Everest. So, head out into your local area with the intention of making up your own routes. You might climb a tree in a wood and name your climb the Awesome Ash Ascent. Or climb up to the top of the slide using an unconventional route, naming it something like the North Face of the 'Rec' Slide.

## CLIMB... IN PLAYGROUNDS

Traversing on playground climbing walls is great practice for route-finding and getting a strong grip. Challenge yourself and others to traverse a route in the fastest time possible. Make it harder by 'banning' certain holds. If there are a few of you, play Shark Attack: mill around facing the climbing wall. Someone is chosen as the shark and whenever 'Shark Attack' is shouted, everyone has to get onto the wall and hang on. The last one off the ground is 'eaten' by the shark and is out. See who survives the longest.

# DO COLLECT SOMETHING

Whether its football cards, stamps, coins, badges or teapots, creating collections of interesting items, whether common or rare, will provide satisfying memories of places that you have visited.

The idea of starting a collection, whether long-lasting or short-lived for one occasion, should appeal to your child's interests. The location you visit can provide some ideas of what you might want to collect, e.g. leaves in a woodland, pebbles on a beach etc.

Some locations do not encourage you to take things away, so be aware and respectful of where you go and what you choose to collect.

### COLLECT... FOSSILS AND GEMSTONES

Treasure can often be hidden in caves, rocks and cliffs on hillsides and coastlines in the form of fossils or gemstones. Take along a few simple tools (e.g. a butter knife) and with some keen eyesight you might spot fossils protruding out of the rocks. If you take any findings along to a fossil and gem shop, they should be able to identify what you have collected.

### COLLECT... CONKERS

Generations of children have collected conkers during autumn with the aim of playing this popular playground game. Part of the fun is finding a blanket of fallen horse chestnut seeds on the ground and prising open the husks to reveal the glossy treasure inside. Choose the best ones from your collection, drill holes into them and thread string or shoelaces through, ready to begin the challenge of hitting an opponent's conker to smithereens.

### BEAT THE CLOCK

Don't wait till you get home to drill the conkers and play the game. Take the tools along with you and do it there and then! NOTE Children love using tools and should be encouraged to do so sensibly with supervision.

## COLLECT... LEAVES

In autumn when the leaves are changing and falling off the trees, they form a wonderful array of shapes, sizes and colours. Wander through a woodland or forest and collect a variety of leaves. Try to find out the names of the trees that the leaves are from. Later you could turn this into a matching/pairs game. Alternatively, display your collection by creating a picture or a collage. Don't forget to take along some art equipment to help with this, such as paper and glue.

## COLLECT... PEBBLES OR SHELLS

While wandering along a beach or riverbank, spend some time beachcombing or gazing down at the shore. Keep an eye out for any interesting shells or pebbles to collect. Use the shells to make a mobile, wind-chime or jewellery. Your collection of pebbles can be used to create a piece of natural art (see page 54).

# DO  CREATE

Get those creative juices flowing by working with natural materials outdoors. Remember, it's the process and not the end product that's important, so let your offspring experiment and be as creative as they want.

Getting the whole family involved adds to the fun, as you all work together to create unique and wonderful arty projects, some of which can be taken home as memories of your mini-adventure and some of which can be left to inspire (and entertain) others.

### CREATE... ICE BAUBLES

Head out into the cold winter weather (ideally below zero), when many of the trees are bare and create your own ice baubles. Collect natural objects from the floor such as acorns, pine needles and berries. Fill a small bowl or plate with water and add the collected objects. You can add food colouring too for a splash of colour. Don't forget to add string so that you can tie up your baubles. Leave the water to freeze and once frozen solid remove from the container and hang from nearby trees.

### CREATE... RAIN-WASHED CLOTHING

You'll need to do this activity on a day when the weather forecast is for rain. Take an old t-shirt or vest with you (ideally white or pale-coloured) and some felt-tip pens. Create your colourful design on the material – keep it simple for the best effect. Peg it up in trees or bushes and wait for the rain to do its job. The colours will run and blend to create a wonderful rainbow effect.

### CREATE... A LEAF COLLAGE

In the autumn when there is an array of different-coloured leaves falling off the trees, spend time collecting them, then create your own masterpiece for others to admire.

## CREATE... STICK WEAVING

This activity involves weaving with natural materials and uses sticks for the frame. You can use either four sticks joined to make a square frame, or look for a fork-shaped stick on the woodland floor. Wind wool around the frame in a zigzag pattern and tie at the end. Then look for natural objects such as leaves, flowers and seeds, and weave them in.

## CREATE... BEACH ART

Using natural materials such as pebbles, shells, driftwood and seaweed, create a picture in the sand. Get the whole family to join in, to create a gallery of pictures.

# DO   CYCLE OR SCOOTER

A midweek ride that is less about miles and more about smiles 'wheelie' is a fun way to have a mini-adventure.

An evening cycle ride with the kids doesn't necessarily mean a gruelling slog covering massive distances. In fact, more fun can probably be had in your local area by being creative and doing something on the kids' level. Short, fun-focussed activities work well for all ages (young and elderly) and are perfect for getting to see and know your locality in a different way. Keeping it local makes it more accessible and easier too (no car needed to transport the bikes) and, therefore, more likely to happen.

For parents who are willing to entertain the idea of going for a scooter ride, scooters should also be considered as a form of family transport – particularly in built-up areas where paths and pavements are smooth. Scooters have the added benefit of being small enough to take on public transport, opening up the possibility of linear journeys where the outward or return leg sees you catching a local bus.

**Adults be warned.** Scootering is very more-ish, possibly because it brings the child out of you.

### CYCLE... FAST VERSUS SLOW

Plan a cycle or scooter route around your locality, one that you will complete twice (but not necessarily on the same day). The idea is to razz around the route as fast as you can on one occasion – imitate a hare! Time your journey if you want to. Then, on another occasion, complete the same route as s..l..o..w..l..y as possible – like a tortoise. Compare the experiences using your own criteria to determine which journey was the 'best'.

### CYCLE... TO BE GREENER

Try to use your bike or scooter to make a journey normally made by car. It might be a weekly journey to Scouts or Guides or something similar. It might be a trip to a relative's house for a catch up. It might be to get some bits and bobs from the local shop. It doesn't matter what really. Simply leave the car at home and travel by pedal/push power. Be greener; feel better.

### BEAT THE CLOCK

For any adventure that requires following a route, plan the route on maps ahead of time using Google maps, so that on the day you don't waste any valuable time.

## CYCLE... TO EAT OUT

You need only a small rucksack to be able to fit in all you need to cook a one-pot meal: a stove, a pan, a few ingredients. Pop it all in your bag the night before for a quick getaway and then you are all set for a tasty alfresco adventure. See recipes on pages 114–123.

## CYCLE... TO BECOME MORE STREET-WISE

Take a look at a map of your local area and find a street or road that is completely unfamiliar to you, then set off to find and explore it; consciously get to know it by looking around spotting and noticing things. Then do it again... and again.

# DO EXPLORE

**Exploration and discovery are available to everyone; well, everyone who puts their mind to it, that is.**

Exploration – to travel and learn about new places – need not be restricted to bearded adventurers. Our local areas have plenty for our beardless youngsters to explore and learn about. And exploration doesn't have to be a massively time-consuming practice or be something that costs a lot of money and requires a lot of specialist equipment. No, being an explorer is more about having a particular mindset, an inquiring mind. Encouraging a child to explore develops an inquiring mind and nurtures someone that is interested and engaged in the world around them. And that's no bad thing, is it?

### EXPLORE... YOUR GARDEN
Exploring your garden – unless it is huge or you've just moved house – will require a bit of imagination for it to feel different or exciting. One idea is to explore it from a pet's perspective. Let your pet out (but maybe not if it's a bird, or is wild and dangerous) and then follow it around, ideally at its own eye level. See which parts of the garden it finds interesting and think about why that is.

### EXPLORE... SOME WOODLAND
Take a football into a woodland and let the ball lead the adventure! Simply take it in turns to kick the ball as far as you can. Follow the moving ball – great fun when it's going downhill – until it stops. When it does stop, look around, listen, smell and feel the surroundings for a few minutes. Then, the ball is kicked again and off you go. It's a fun way to explore an area.

### EXPLORE... A STREET
Go and explore a local street to see if there is any 'treasure' or more accurately, geocaches, hidden (see page 70). All you need is an app and a data connection and you're away. Follow the etiquette of 'caching' though and be discreet, so that Muggles (non-cachers) don't notice what you are doing!

## EXPLORE... A NATURE RESERVE

Walk quietly around the reserve playing 'I spy with my little eye' based on the animals and plants/flowers living in the reserve ecosystem.

## EXPLORE... A CEMETERY

Respectfully explore a cemetery and learn about your local area from the information on gravestones and commemorative statues. Find the grave of the oldest person buried and think about/find out about their name. Deduce whether any local men or women died in battle serving their country. Make some wax crayon rubbings of ornate carvings or etchings. Cemeteries can be fascinating and thought-provoking places to explore.

# DO FEED

Give nature a helping hand by offering our feathered, furry and prickly friends a tasty meal.

During the winter months, birds, squirrels and hedgehogs can sometimes find it difficult to source food in their natural habitats. So, as you venture out to a different location, near or far, think about which creatures might be sharing it with you and whether you can help out, by taking along some appropriate food for them. Find out what they eat naturally and any offerings you can give them that can help, not harm them. If you do this regularly, your diners will become accustomed to the free food supply and you can guarantee sightings.

## FEED... THE HEDGEHOGS

Sadly, the number of hedgehogs is on the decline and it's important that we do our bit to help them. If you are privileged enough to see one of these prickly visitors, then help them out with a meal. Alternatively, venture out into a nearby woodland or meadow where some have been spotted.

Their natural diet is snails, slugs, earthworms, caterpillars and beetles, making them a welcome visitor to gardens. Crushed cat biscuits or dried mealworms are ideal snacks to help out their diet because they do not freeze or go off quickly. Place fresh mince or dog/cat food (not fish-based) outside, but remove before it goes off and attracts rats.

## FEED... THE BIRDS

Feeding birds is a favourite family pastime – there's even a Mary Poppins song about it! So, during the winter months, head into the garden, a woodland or meadow and take along some ingredients to make bird feeders. Heat up some lard, mix in some bird seed and, as it starts to cool, shape the mixture into balls so that you can attach them to trees and bushes with string.

If you're heading to a lake or a pond where there are waterfowl, think carefully about taking bread. White bread is the 'McDonald's of the pond world, containing large amounts of protein and few nutrients. Vitamin and mineral deficiencies can cause deformed bones and feathers that stick out, preventing birds from being able to fly. Duck food, bought from shops, is a much better option.

## FEED... THE SQUIRRELS

Squirrels naturally forage for food in the woodland and forests that they inhabit, favouring acorns, hazelnuts, pine cones, fungi, bark and roots. While they are independent feeders, storing food for themselves, squirrels may guarantee you a sighting if you can offer extra food such as peanuts.

# DO FILM

## 'Lights, camera, adventure!'

The modern smartphone doubles up as a high quality camera, a piece of highly accessible and mobile pocket-sized technology that offers all sorts of creative possibilities. Photo-manipulation and video-editing apps make it possible to film, edit and share photographs and movies, all with the click of just a few buttons.

This outdoor activity idea is about learning how to use a camera to tell a story, be it an adventure film or a factual documentary. It's not so much about the end product, but the process: learning how to compose shots, how to create linked sequences and how to tell a visual story.

Your global multimillion online audience is waiting for your films and photo galleries, so get your camera at the ready – it's time for some serious 'action'!

### FILM... LINK SEQUENCES
Before making a full-blown film, practise filming a short sequence of events that can be linked together. It could be a short journey on a bike or scooter – the simpler the better. Try taking a variety of shots: a wide shot (of the context); some close-up shots (details); a few shots taken from the rider's point of view (**POV** shots) such as from a head camera or with the camera held in one hand (if it is safe to do so). Remember to keep the camera as still as possible for crisp, clear footage. Start and end on a wide shot when editing the film, and keep it short, one minute in total.

### BEAT THE CLOCK
Plan your film in advance and make a checklist of the shots you need. It will make the filming process more efficient.

## FILM... AN ADVENTURE GENRE FILM

Adventure films tend to have lots of action in them, so think of an adventure you could film that is full of exciting activity. It might be a mountain bike ride or a trail run. Think about the variety of shots you need to capture – see opposite – and keep your eyes open to see where best to capture the footage you need. Try to be creative and experiment with new angles and shots; remember to keep the camera as still as possible. Rather than make lots of sweeping shots (where the camera pans left or right), film short clips that can be used to 'cut' to a different viewpoint.

## FILM... A SHORT DOCUMENTARY

Tell a factual story about a local area or issue. Consider interviewing someone and record a voiceover (a sound track of you talking) over the film clips to help tell the story.

## DO  FLY SOMETHING

Is it a bird? Is it a plane? Is it a kite? Is it a balloon? No, it's... well actually, it doesn't matter what it is, just go and fly something!

This activity is all about location, location, location. In order to fly a kite, plane or balloon, you need space and plenty of it. You certainly don't want to be tripping up, or spending time untangling your flying objects from trees.

So, choose a wide, open space away from electricity cables, roads and obstacles such as buildings or trees; look for spaces such as parks, fields or beaches.

Some wind is good. Too much will probably spoil the fun!

### FLY... A PLANE
Take along some paper (ideally reuse scrap paper) and pens or crayons. Spend some time folding the planes and decorate them in your own personalised style. Once everyone has their own plane(s), experiment by launching them. Try to see whose plane flies the furthest or does the fanciest tricks (deliberately or not!). You can buy packs of polystyrene planes that are quick and easy to make and cheap to buy. They are tougher than paper planes, so probably better for the outdoors. But they don't recycle!

### FLY... RADIO-CONTROLLED VEHICLES
Micro drones and helicopters make great toys, and children enjoy learning how these machines work. Best flown outside in open spaces, they are a great incentive to get the kids into the fresh air.

## FLY... SOME BUBBLES

Young children love bubbles. And let's face it, even the oldies do too. Take along some bubble mix (bought or made) and a wand. You can get giant bubble wands for wow factor. Take turns making the bubbles while everyone else chases them and pops them.

Bubble recipe: 1 part washing-up liquid (good quality) to 10 parts water. 3 parts glycerine (available from chemists) is optional.

You can make a wand from a coathanger or garden wire, but be careful of sharp ends!

## FLY... A KITE

Flying a kite is great fun on a windy day. You don't have to be an expert to fly a simple kite and part of the fun is in the learning! Working as a team adds to the overall enjoyment. If you aren't the one holding the string, you can help launch the kite by running along with it and then easing it into the air.

While you're waiting for a blustery day, how about making a kite or a ribbon banner?

A ribbon banner is a simpler alternative to a kite; easier for children to make and to fly.

## DO  FOLLOW

Follow the yellow brick road, or any other trail for that matter;  it may be good for your heart (and soul).

Kids love to play 'follow the leader' type games – as leader or follower, it doesn't matter – and this kind of game can be extended in different ways and applied to different scenarios. Various locations offer trails to follow and you can even be inventive and create your own.

Following a trail, or following someone who is following a trail, is a fun thing to do and it has the added benefit of being a good form of outdoor exercise – even if it might leave you a little hot and sweaty!

### FOLLOW... AN OUTDOOR GYM

Playgrounds often have outdoor gyms attached to them where children and adults can 'work out'. The gyms don't offer a given circuit, so you will need to create your own programme of activities to follow, to ensure you exercise a range of different muscles. Pace yourself and aim to complete the circuit three times. Repeat your training over a period of weeks to see noticeable increases in your strength and stamina.

### FOLLOW... A TRIM TRAIL

Following trim trails are a good way of improving your strength and balance – they are good fun too, as it feels as though you are playing more than anything else. Try and complete the trim trail without touching the ground. If you do put a foot down, start the particular obstacle or activity again (or maybe even the full trail).

### FOREST TRAIL

Follow a forest trail on foot or mountain bike, or leave the path and create your own route. Leave some natural signs of your route (arrows made from twigs or scratch marks in the ground) for others to follow.

### TOWN TRAIL

Digital trails are an excellent means of exploring and learning about your local area or a place you are visiting. You'll need a smartphone on which to download and follow the trail. Some trails include audio and video clips that bring the content to life.

### BEAT THE CLOCK

Download the digital trail beforehand – this saves you having to reply on a data connection. Some trails include **PDF** worksheets or maps to print out and take with you.

# DO  FORAGE

Enjoy nature's own garden – get out and pick some ingredients for tasty treats.

Food always tastes better when cooked with fresh ingredients and is all the more rewarding if you've grown or picked some of those ingredients yourself. From late spring to autumn, a range of fruits and plants are available to pick in various locations, from woodland to hedgerows and open fields. If you are planning to go foraging while out and about, why not cook your hoard at the same time, adding wild garlic to your meal, strawberries to your Eton mess or freshly stewed blackberries to scones, yoghurt or porridge oats?

**N.B.** Remember that you aren't the only people out and about; when picking, avoid areas low to the ground which dogs might have used for a toilet!

### GO FORAGING... FOR STRAWBERRIES

The strawberry season is late spring into summer. Rather than buy strawberries from the shops, spend some time picking enough to fill a few punnets, in the sunshine from the numerous PYO (Pick Your Own) farms that pop up at this time of year. Once you have collected a punnet or two (and maybe eaten a punnet or two as well), reward yourself by making an instant homemade dessert. Take along some clotted cream and meringues. Crush the meringues and mix them with chopped strawberries and clotted cream for a quick Eton mess.

### GO FORAGING... FOR BLACKBERRIES

Blackberries, or brambles, begin to appear in the hedgerows or sunny patches in woodlands in late summer and early autumn. When you head out for a walk to a woodland or meadow look out for brambles – be warned, it can be addictive! Wear some old clothes and trousers to protect your legs from the thorns and take along a container to collect them in. You can either take them home for cooking, or make an instant compôte in situ by washing them and stewing them with sugar.

### BEAT THE CLOCK

Have containers in a bag for your collections. Pack a gas stove, pan and some sugar and you'll be fully prepared to cook your harvest too.

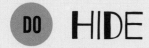

# DO  HIDE

**Whether you're looking for hidden treasure, secret notes or surprises, you'll find it difficult to hide your excitement!**

Treasure hunts, Easter egg hunts and hide and seek are all popular childhood games that never go out of fashion. The thrill of hiding something secret appeals to adults and children alike, in the same way that finding hidden treasure provides a thrill of unexpected excitement. So if you're not busy hunting for eggs or playing hide and seek, try a couple of alternative activities to get you outdoors in the search for new or favourite locations in which to hide things.

### HIDE... A NOTE

No, not a bank note (unless you're feeling generous!). Try hiding a written note in a secret location that only you know about. Write on the note a mini 'bucket list' of what you would like to do/achieve in a given time, e.g. a year. After the given time, return to the same spot, find the hidden note and see what you have (or have not) achieved. You could write your New Year's Resolutions on a note, then return on New Year's Day a year later to see if you kept to them!

### HIDE... A BAG OF SURPRISES

Here's a game that will encourage you to take a closer look at the location you are in. Each of you should take a small fabric bag and as you wander around, collect five or six items to place inside. The fun begins when you take it in turns to delve into someone else's bag (without looking) and try to guess what the items are. Don't forget to put them back afterwards.

### HIDE... A GEOCACHE

Geocaching is a popular modern treasure hunt that requires a smartphone/GPS with a downloadable app with which to locate hidden treasure (or caches) in all sorts of places. Rather than try to find a geocache, why not hide one for other people to find? Choose a suitable container that can withstand all weather conditions. In your container, put a notepad, pencil and a small miscellaneous item (treasure). Once at your location, look around for a good place to hide your container, so that it is not immediately obvious. There are some guidelines to follow on Geocache websites that you would be wise to check. Once you've chosen your hideaway, record the GPS coordinates using your smartphone or GPS.

### BEAT THE CLOCK

You'll need to be prepared for this activity and have downloaded the app, sorted out a container and contents, and carried out some research on suitable locations.

# DO INVESTIGATE

It's science kids, but not as you know it. No white lab coats required, just an inquiring mind.

Science is often thought to be a subject that is studied indoors (in a science lab) or by the super-intelligent or stereotypical mad professor types. But, actually, science – or 'understanding the world we live in'– is for everyone. And learning about scientific things can take place anywhere, especially outdoors, where the natural world can be investigated and interpreted in an engaging, hands-on way.

Getting outdoors and investigating the natural world can take place at any time of the year. Nature is constantly in a state of flux as the weather, temperature, light, wind, and the habits of the inhabitants of ecosystems change dynamically. There is always something to observe and investigate, and doing so on a regular basis helps us to understand the world in which we live and become more in tune with it.

Getting outside and learning to appreciating nature is also good for our minds and our general well-being.

## INVESTIGATE... THE WEATHER

The natural world can give us important clues as to what the weather is going to be like. But before you rely too heavily on what the cows or birds are telling us, do some investigating:

Cows lying down – do they do this before it's going to rain?
Cows lying together – does this mean bad weather is on the way?
Pine cones – do they open when the air is dry and close when the air is humid?
Do birds go quiet just before it rains?
Are there lots of birds on the power lines? What might this mean?
'Flowers smell best just before rain.' Is this proverb accurate?

Study the nature in your local area carefully and see if you can come up with some of your own predictors.

## INVESTIGATE... WATER

Puddles – carefully draw around the outside of a puddle with a piece of chalk and repeat again after 15 minutes, 30 minutes and one hour. What has happened to the puddle? Where has the water gone? It has evaporated into the air. What affects the rate of puddle shrinkage? Heat, humidity, wind? Use this investigation to state what sort of day is a good day to hang out the washing.

## INVESTIGATE... A MURDER SCENE

Find a dead animal or insect and investigate clues as to how it died.

## INVESTIGATE... A STREAM

Drop a twig into a stream in different places: inside of a bend (meander), outside of a bend, shallow water and deep water. Investigate and explain why the speed of the movement of the twig varies.

## INVESTIGATE... BUGS

Walk carefully through a wood or forest looking for mini-beasts like spiders, insects and woodlice (you may need to turn a log or two, or move a stone).

## INVESTIGATE... GREEN LEAVES

Make your initials using small pieces of black card, then carefully paper-clip them to a green leaf (growing on a tree/plant). Come back a few days later and remove the card. What has happened to the leaf and why? (It's to do with chlorophyll.)

# DO LEARN (SOMETHING NEW)

Learn something new every day and, in a year's time you'll have learned... well, 365 things. And if you didn't already know that, then there's one thing you've learned already!

Learning something new is very empowering, be it a trick, a skill or a new bit of knowledge – it doesn't matter. Helping a child to learn about the outdoors – to understand it, appreciate it and enjoy it – is one of the best gifts we can give. As with all learning, the important part is the process – the doing, having a go, persevering until you get it – not the end product itself, so try to refrain from doing too much for the learner and don't fret if the finished product or outcome isn't perfect. Encourage and praise determination, effort and motivation to complete something to the best of one's ability. Do this and both the learner and 'guide at their side' will enjoy the process and feel good about it.

### LEARN... HOW TO MAKE A ROPE SWING

Don't rely on other people's rope swings, learn how to make your own. Take a length of rope and tie a bowline (see opposite) at the end. Throw the rope over a strong and healthy limb of a tree and then feed the end through the loop and pull it (so the bowline works its way upwards). Get a strong branch and secure it to the end of your rope using a double constrictor knot to give you a secure seat. Then swing!

### BEAT THE CLOCK

Cut a short length of rope that your child can use indoors or on journeys to practise knot tying – it'll make the swing-making process quicker, leaving more time to swing.

### LEARN... HOW TO IDENTIFY HAZEL

Hazel is a fast-growing tree that is perfect for a range of outdoor bushcraft-style activities – such as whittling and fuel for fires. Learn how to identify it from its catkins, seeds (hazelnuts of course) and leaves. Hazel grows vertically straight when coppiced at ground level, so this is another method of identifying a hazel tree.

## LEARN... HOW TO TIE A KNOT

**REEF KNOT** This is good for tying together two bits of rope/cord (of equal thickness). Remember the technique by: left over right – and under – right over left – and under.

**CLOVE HITCH** A good binding knot for starting/finishing lashings.

**BOWLINE** Useful for fixing a loop at the end of a rope. Remember the technique by making a loop (rabbit hole) then saying, 'Up through the rabbit hole, round the big tree, down through the rabbit hole and off goes he'.

**DOUBLE CONSTRICTOR KNOT** Similar to a clove hitch, but much more robust and reliable.

## LEARN... HOW TO MAKE A TASTY S'MORE

A tasty campfire treat popular in Canada and the US composed of marshmallow, biscuit and chocolate. Sounds nice, yeah? Learn how to make one (see page 123) or invent your own 's'more-ish' campfire treat.

## DOUBLE CONSTRICTOR KNOT

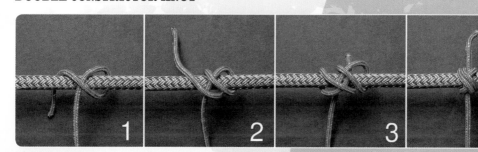

## CLOVE HITCH

## BOWLINE

# DO **LOOK AROUND**

Life can sometimes be very hectic, leaving little time to simply look around, absorb the atmosphere, admire the view or observe the actions of others. So, stop and look around for a while!

This activity does not require a lot of 'doing'; you can just sit, while everyone else does the work and you merely watch and learn (or be entertained).

What you actually look at will depend on the location. While walking in the local area, city centre and nearby streets, there'll be traffic and people around you to look at. Rather than accept what is happening around you, look around – really spend time scanning the scene and focussing on individuals. If the location is rural and there are no vehicles or people around, then focus on the scenery.

### LOOK AROUND... AT THE LANDSCAPE

When you find a beautiful location, you want to soak up the view. Bring out the artist in you and focus on the colours and shapes of the scene before you. Take along some binoculars so that you can see beyond what the naked eye can make out. Also, take along a sketchbook and record the scene. You don't have to be a good artist; whatever you produce will form a memory for you.

### LOOK AROUND... AT TRAFFIC

Some children have a fascination with (and knowledge of) different types of transport; this activity will therefore appeal to them, but equally so for others. Rather than simply looking at the traffic, turn it into a game.

- Everyone choose a colour and count the coloured vehicles of their chosen colour that pass within a given time. Which colour was most popular?
- Traffic Bingo (with homemade Bingo cards, see below.

### LOOK AROUND... AT PEOPLE

Watching other people can be fascinating, purposeful and even entertaining. Scan a busy street scene and look around at the vast differences between the people – how they look and how they move.

You can also learn a lot by watching others. If the location has people performing different activities, e.g. skateboarders at a skate park, sailors on a lake, surfers at the beach, then spend the time looking and learning. You never know, it might spark a new hobby!

### BEAT THE CLOCK

Create the bingo cards before you go. Draw some 3 x 3 grids on them. Fill the grids with pictures or words for different types of vehicles, e.g. different colours or makes of vehicles or even specific vehicles, e.g. a tractor or a haulage lorry.

# DO LOOK DOWN

Look down – past your smartphone – and enjoy the wonders that are literally beneath our feet.

Looking down, properly, is a bit over-rated these days. Sure, people (adults and children alike) do spend a lot of time looking down at their smartphones and tablets, but looking beyond these devices is probably not on most people's radars as something to do and enjoy. This is a shame, because the detail and delights that the real world has to offer are often much more captivating and enlightening than the pixelated virtual world we gaze into.

This mini-adventure activity aims to reinstate the thrill of looking down – at ground level – as a cool 'must-do' thing.

### LOOK DOWN... AT TRACKS AND FOOTPRINTS

Famous bushcraft expert Ray Mears once used his tracking skills to find a criminal on the run. Develop your skills by looking carefully for signs that tell you someone, or something, has been there before you. Look for: broken plant stems, trampled grass, drops of water on the banks of streams, discarded items and, of course, footprints or tracks.

### LOOK DOWN... AT OWL PELLETS

Many birds produce pellets (small sausage-shaped objects containing the indigestible materials of their diet, such as bones, insect body parts, teeth, claws etc., as well as some softer materials like fur and vegetable fibres). If you look down carefully under feeding posts or roosts, you might be lucky enough to find a pellet that an owl has passed through its mouth. If you find one, dissect it using tweezers and a magnifying glass, and deduce what sort of meals the bird has been enjoying recently.

### BEAT THE CLOCK

Gather together a magnifying glass, tweezers and maybe even a knife to take with you so they are at hand should you find a pellet.

## LOOK DOWN AT...
## CRACKS AND CREVICES

Our pavements and footpaths are full of cracks and crevices, so look down to avoid turning your ankle and, more interestingly, to see whether Mother Nature has exploited the opportunity. Look for growing weeds or flowers, or tiny holes made by insects.

## LOOK DOWN AT...
## HOLES AND BURROWS

Holes in the ground are often intentionally made by something. Stop (at an appropriate distance depending on the hole) and watch for activity – it might be a scuttling beetle, a trail of ants or even a mammal of some kind if you are observing a burrow.

# DO  LOOK UNDER

Looking under something can reveal a whole new world – albeit quite a small one, so look carefully, and with patience.

This adventure idea is really simple and easy to do. It will hopefully give you a new perspective on the world beneath, whether it's under a log, under water or looking at something under a microscope. And, because it is likely that a lot of things you'll see will be small, this adventure encourages attention to detail and tuning into a world that often feels so far removed, even though it always exists beneath us.

## LOOK UNDER... A LENS

You only need a cheap magnifying glass or microscope to be able to see the tiny world below in glorious magnification. You may need a pooter (bug container) to capture critters so that getting them under the microscope is a bit easier. Make sure you release them back as soon as you can though, to prevent them from getting too stressed.

## LOOK UNDER... WATER

The smallest of ponds is likely to be teeming with life, and rock pools are amazing places to look into. Make yourself a rough-and-ready tick list of things you hope to spot, such as:

POND Beetles, larvae, water fleas, amphibians, dragonflies and damselflies, snails, shrimps and, of course, small fish.

ROCK POOL Starfish, shrimp, sea anemone, sea urchin, limpet, mussel, crab, hermit crab, fish.

## BEAT THE CLOCK

Get a small net and a plastic tray ready, along with an identification sheet for the section of water that you are going to look at. You might need to search for one online and print it out.

## LOOK UNDER... BUSHES AND HEDGEROWS

Explore under bushes and hedgerows, as they too will be bustling with life, especially during the warmer months of the year. You could perhaps make a simple hedgehog shelter in the summer months and return later in the year to see if a hedgehog has used it for its hibernation. Take care not to disturb anything that is sleeping though.

## LOOK UNDER... A LOG OR STONE

This is easy to do because logs and stones are everywhere and the chances are you'll find something living underneath them. It's a bit mind-boggling to think that things live in the tiny space between a rock or log and the ground, but some mini-beasts like the damp, dark and 'tight' conditions such places afford. Take a moment to watch and study the little critters living there before carefully putting their shelter back in place. Look carefully under larger objects and you may catch a glimpse of a snake or a slow worm.

# DO LOOK UP

Look into the night sky and wish upon a shooting star, or a planet, or a satellite, or... well, anything else you might be able to see.

The best way to enjoy the night sky is to sit down and make oneself as comfortable as possible. This goes against the notion of adventure to some degree, but, on this occasion, comfort will enhance the experience. Basically, the warmer and more comfortable you are, the longer you can endure the potentially cold temperatures, and therefore see more.

A few pieces of technology and kit such as a night sky app on your smartphone and

some decent astronomical binoculars and tripod will also enhance the experience.

The last piece of the puzzle is finding the right location in which to base oneself – somewhere as high as possible, with uninterrupted views and minimal light pollution. Oh, and then there's the weather, but you can't do much about that except keep an eye on the local forecast.

### LOOK UP TO... THE MOON
The Moon is Earth's only natural satellite, some 384,400 km (238,900 miles) away and orbiting Earth every 27 days. It rotates at the same rate as it orbits Earth, so we only ever see one side of it.

### BEAT THE CLOCK
Research and install (and get familiar with) any apps you plan to use to enhance the night sky-watching experience at least a day or two before you head out – it will save you lots of messing around on the night.

## LOOK UP TO... THE STARS

Stars, like our sun, are hot bodies of glowing gas. There are billions of stars in the universe and one of the most spectacular sites to try and observe is the Milky Way – the galaxy that our solar system is part of. Look for a milky arch across the night sky.

## LOOK UP TO... SATELLITES

Man-made satellites orbit Earth providing us with TV, radio and GPS signals. They look like tiny stars ,but they can be seen moving – very quickly. The International Space Station (ISS) orbits Earth more than 15 times a day and is visible with the naked eye. Use an app to find out where and when to look out for it.

## LOOK UP TO...  THE PLANETS

Five of the planets in our solar system can be seen with the naked eye, they are: Mercury, Venus, Mars, Jupiter and Saturn. Without a powerful telescope they will just look like bright stars, although some colour might be noticed (red from Mars for instance). Their places in the night sky vary though – as they orbit the Sun – so use an app to help you identify them with confidence.

## LOOK UP TO... SHOOTING STARS

Shooting stars are not stars at all, but the visible path of a meteoroid as it burns up in the earth's atmosphere. Look carefully at the night sky towards the horizon and be patient. When you see one, make a wish.

# DO MAKE

**Make time to be creative, then be creative with what you make.**

We live in a materialistic world and are losing many of the skills to make our own tools or materials that might have been passed down through generations before us. With a bit of time and patience, something we often lack, we can make all sorts of things.

If you have ever had a hankering to make or learn a skill, particularly in the outdoors, make the time, follow your passion and just do it. You may be curious to take on a new challenge and learning with others is fun.

## MAKE... A BUTTER KNIFE

Take along some bushcraft tools (saw and knife) and head into a forest or woodland. Look for long, thin sticks; hazel stems are ideal because they often grow straight and have multiple stems, plus if you saw one off at ground level (at 45° so the water runs off) more will soon grow back. After sawing off your stick (with adult supervision), whittle a flat end using a knife (once again with adult supervision). Round off the top corners for a professional look.

## MAKE... SOME CORDAGE

There's plenty of natural stuff out there that you can use to make cordage, e.g. nettles, brambles and wood, such as willow. The fibres inside the stems or bark are what is needed to make rope. After removing the outer layer (thorns, stinging hairs or bark) you need to strip the fibres and allow them to dry before twisting the fibres to make cordage. More detailed information can be found in books or online, but this is a rewarding activity for the outdoors.

## MAKE... A TREASURE HUNT

While at your chosen location, draw a map of the area, marking on key features and adding a key. Then turn the map into a treasure map by hiding some treasure and marking its location on the map.

Why not turn your map into a jigsaw map and give it to someone? Stick the map on the back of a picture, then cut the picture up into pieces (don't make it too difficult!). Put all the pieces into an envelope and send it to someone or give it to them in person.

## BEAT THE CLOCK

Carry out some research and practise the techniques before you head out to make your rope.

# DO PADDLE

When the weather is fine, you know it's a sign, for messing about on the river.

Often you don't have to venture far (or at all) from a town and city to find a waterside location; rivers, canals and centrally located parks with small lakes all offer an escape from the hubbub of modern life. Alternatively, you may go to a nearby lake or beach. Whichever location you choose, think about heading onto the water for some family fun. Where there is water, there are often water sport outlets that allow you to hire various vessels if you don't have your own, or maybe a nice friend can lend you one. Depending on what you choose, you may need other equipment such as wetsuits too.

## PADDLE... A PEDALO

Most people associate pedalos with holidays at the coast or abroad but who says you have to wait until the holidays? These fun, plastic floating pedalled craft can sometimes be hired on boating lakes as well as at the beach. Share the hard work and take turns pedalling.

## PADDLE... A ROWING BOAT

The rowing boat is not often the most popular choice for messing about on the water but many laughs can be had trying to row a boat in a straight line! A rowing boat can also hold a group of people and is a sturdy vessel on the water.

## PADDLE... A CANOE/KAYAK

Canoes and kayaks can be easily hired from water sport centres at various locations. Both can be paddled in pairs, with an adult and child teaming up, and canoes can hold three adults or two adults and two children.

## PADDLE... A SUP

Stand Up Paddleboarding has become an increasingly popular sport. Boards and paddles can be hired from water sport outlets or purchased from sports shops. Their large size means that they can accommodate an adult and child, or two children working together. Chances are you will get wet doing this, so wear wetsuits. If new to the sport, choose flat water rather than battle with waves.

# DO  PERFORM

**The world is your stage, so get out there and perform in a variety of different places.**

Music and theatre are often performed in the open air during the summer months as audiences venture outside to position themselves on the grassy banks of hillsides, rivers and open spaces, ready to watch their favourite musicians and actors do their thing. If you have some budding artistes, encourage them to take their art into the great outdoors for a family performance. Whether it's singing, dancing, storytelling or stage fighting, encourage them to spend time practising and refining their performance before the final show. Time can be spent preparing the performance and any props before the day of the performance at your chosen location.

### PERFORM... A SHADOW PUPPET SHOW

Shadow puppets are an ancient Chinese art form which use amazing, intricate puppets to tell a story. Your budding storytellers can also create their own puppets to take along on your mini family adventure. Take along a sheet to perform behind; position the sheet so that the sun is behind the performers. Alternatively, use torchlight as your light source. Ensure that you have plenty of time to practise before the performance.

### BEAT THE CLOCK

Make the puppets before you go. Cut out chosen shapes from black card and attach long sticks on to the back. You will need to have an idea of the story that you are going to tell in order to have the right characters.

### PERFORM... A FIGHT SEQUENCE

Dramatic action shots in films are recorded in unusual and spectacular locations. They require a lot of rehearsing so that all of the actors know what is going to happen and when. At your chosen location, spend some time creating your fight sequence – the more time you spend on it, the more realistic it will look! Don't forget to record the final performance.

## PERFORM... A DANCE

There is plenty of space in the outdoors. Take along some music and allow your dance enthusiasts to create a dance to perform to the rest of the family.

## PERFORM... A POEM

If your performer is less physical or athletic, they may want to perform a poem instead. Everyone in the family could perform a different poem or work together to say different parts.

# DO PLANT

Plant seeds (or ideas) and they might grow into bigger things!

Wildflowers and trees naturally disperse their seeds and will find new places to grow, but sometimes they need a helping hand. The benefits are not only for them, but also the wildlife that relies on them. You don't need to be a keen gardener or horticulturist to plant wildflower seeds, but you will need to have an awareness of where the flowers might grow most successfully.

If you have your own garden or allotment the process will take longer as you see the planting through to the harvesting and eating stage. Growing food can be a great project that involves the whole family.

### PLANT... A SEED
Create a wild corner in your garden. Buy a packet of wildflower seeds (native) and plant them in your chosen spot. You'll then be able to watch them grow and see the insects that are attracted to them. Try to learn the names of some common flowers so that you'll be able to recognize them when you're out and about.

### PLANT... A TREE
We all know trees are important and good for us as well as wildlife. Trees play an important role in reducing climate change, provide a habitat for insects, birds and animals and make our environments better places to live in. So, the more the better! Find a suitable spot to plant a young sapling and you'll be doing your bit to help.

### PLANT... FRUIT AND VEGETABLES
Growing your own fruit and vegetables is rewarding, not only because you get to eat your produce, but also because it gives you a good understanding of how plants grow. Find out which plants will grow best in your garden or allotment then dedicate some time to sowing, tending and harvesting your crops. This is obviously a longer-term project that requires an investment of time.

## DO  PLAY

**End the day with lots of time to play!**

Children love to play and, let's face it, adults do too – we just have to make time to escape the screens and the sedentary lifestyle for some good old family fun in the outdoors. Playing together as a family is a great way to relieve stress, relax and bond together as a unit, creating shared memories. The games that you play will not only quicken the heart rate but also promote social skills such as turn-taking and coping with both winning and losing fairly. So when out exploring, make time to play a game together. We all need to make time to play; it should be a necessity rather than a luxury.

### PLAY... FRENCH CRICKET
One person is a batsman and everyone else is fielding. The object of the game is to get the batsman out by hitting him/her on the leg or catching him/her out. The batsman must stand holding a cricket bat, in one spot and cannot move. The fielders bowl to the batsman who in turn hits the ball. The fielders can only bowl from the point at which they stop or catch the ball.

### PLAY... BALLOON STOMP
Each person playing the game should attach an inflated balloon to a long piece of string and then attach the end of that string around their ankle. The aim of the game is to stomp on, and pop, everyone else's balloon. You could split into two teams and use two different coloured balloons. Have plenty of spare balloons so that you can keep playing, and don't forget to pick up all your litter at the end.

## PLAY... TAG

There are so many different variations of this game with a wide variety of names too but the basics ultimately remain the same: someone is 'it' and they have to run around chasing everyone else, trying to tag them. If a person is tagged they then become the new 'it'.

### VARIATIONS INCLUDE:

**SHADOW TAG** The person chasing has to stand on someone's shadow rather than tag that person. You need a sunny day to play this version!

**FREEZE TAG** If someone is tagged, they must stand still and wait to be released by the other players.

## PLAY... DODGE BALL

Split into two teams and divide the area into two small sections. Each team member stands in their section and tries to throw balls (soft) at the other team's players, while avoiding being hit. Players are out if they get hit, or if their ball is caught by a member of the other team.

# DO HAVE A RACE

**On your marks, get set ... GO! (and have a race).**

Kids at all stages in life love having races. Races are exciting and, in a strange way, a bit scary – that's probably why they are exciting. They get the heart pumping and the adrenalin rushing and they can be great for developing a competitive spirit, as well as the qualities of being a good sport.

Organising a race as your midweek adventure doesn't have to mean the obvious, and perhaps a little bit dull, running race. We have listed here some kinds of races that are a bit different, ones you may not have considered before.

### RACE AROUND... A BIKE CIRCUIT
Rather than make a circuit and razz around as fast as you can, design a short route that tests your skill and control of your bike e.g. tight turns, over small obstacles, along a balance beam. Decide a scoring system that penalizes a rider who puts their foot down e.g. two points added. The race is then about who can complete the route with the lowest score in the fastest time.

### RACE... STICKS, BOATS AND RAFTS
If there is running water in your locality, then a stick, raft (if you can make one) or toy boat race is a must. Agree on the course, how to begin the race in a fair manner and establish the rules of interference (i.e. if it gets stuck on a rock or branch or in rapids) before the race starts. Always race an odd number of heats (such as best of three or five).

### BEAT THE CLOCK
Make a model raft from twigs that have been lashed together beforehand and have it ready for when race day arrives.

### RACE... SNAILS OR SLUGS
Select a few slimy athletes carefully and race them in their natural environment. Due to their lack of speed it's best to race them over 100mm (4in) not 100m (109yds)!

## RACE TO... PITCH A TENT

Whether or not you intend on camping out for the night, practise putting up and taking down a tent as quickly as you can, making it, ultimately, a timed race. See which family member can gain and retain the fastest time. Being able to put up a tent quickly comes in handy when you go camping in the rain, so this activity doubles up as survival training.

## RACE... AN OBSTACLE COURSE

Woods and forests have everything you need in them to make an awesome obstacle course: logs, branches, mud patches, puddles, swings... you name it. When creating your course, be creative and 'force' participants to go under, over, between, through and along things. Wear old clothes and decent footwear. You might even smear some mud onto your face... for 'go faster' stripes!

# DO REUSE AND RECYCLE

We regularly reuse and recycle rubbish, but have you ever thought about reusing or recycling nature's waste, such as fallen leaves, flowers or seeds? If you haven't, then with a bit of imagination these can be ideal materials to get creative with.

The outdoors offers a free supply of natural art materials. But sometimes, the hardest part of being creative is coming up with the ideas. That's why we've helped you with a few pointers for each season. Your own ideas are likely to be even better than ours. Look around your locality to see what materials are falling from trees and flowers, and use these as your starting point. Remember, there are no right and wrongs when it comes to art.

Be aware of allergies, as some children can be allergic to leaves, flowers and seeds.

### REUSE... BY CREATING A MAGIC POTION

Don't let the beautiful petals that fall from flowers go to waste. Collect them, put them into a small jar with lots of other 'magic' ingredients and make a special – beautifully scented – potion with which to cast some magic spells.

### BEAT THE CLOCK

Collect pine cones in the autumn when they fall to the ground and before they rot. Save them until December when you need them (and when there aren't any to collect).

## RECYCLE... LEAF BUNTING

Collect some nice golden, red, or brown leaves in the autumn. Using some sewing cotton (biodegradable), tie different leaves at regular intervals to make some natural bunting. Tie the bunting on something manmade to make it look more pleasing to the eye.

## REUSE... BY PAINTING A STONE

Using acrylic paints, paint an image on a pebble or stone but keep it simple. Alternatively write a message like 'Good Luck' or 'Happy Birthday'. Varnish the stone with PVA glue or proper varnish.

## RECYCLE... A CHRISTMAS WREATH

Save some money by making a wreath to give to someone. Find a thin birch or willow branch and cut it to size – so you can bend the branch into a circle. Tie the branch with some string to keep its shape and then start weaving holly sprigs and/or small-leaved branches from fir trees around the circle. Finish off your wreath by adding a few pine cones (use some wire – like an old paperclip – to attach the pine cones). An optional extra could be to spray some fake snow or glitter onto your wreath – but go steady as less is more!

# DO  SLIDE

## Slip and slide on sand and snow – sledging all year round!

Sledges often sit unused for a large proportion of the year as we pine for heavy snowfall; however, with a bit of creative thinking, you can get out and sledge at different times of the year and in different locations. A plastic sledge is not an expensive purchase and can be bought from a variety of stores. They come in all shapes and sizes.

When planning a mini-sledging adventure, the location will obviously need to be sloping, so head out to some open hilly fields or sand dunes for the activities below.

Safety precautions should be taken when sledging to avoid injuries; always check that the route is clear ahead and ensure that there are no hidden obstacles that could be dangerous on the slope or at the bottom.

### SLIDE... BY SNOW-SLEDGING
Sledging is synonymous with snow and after a heavy snowfall, families often head out to the nearest slopes to spend a few hours hurtling down hills. When it next snows, clock off and head for the hills with your sledges in tow. Wrap up warm and take some hot chocolate or soup to warm up with after the excitement.

### SLIDE... BY SAND-SLEDGING
You don't need snow to go sledging; try getting out on sand dunes to experience a similar thrill. For a mini-family adventure near home or while on holiday, head to a beach with sand dunes and choose a slope to slide down. Be prepared to get sand everywhere!

N.B. Please check that the sand dunes are free to access and are not out of bounds for any conservation reasons.

## SLIDE... BY GRASS-SLEDGING

Unlike normal sledges, the sledges used on grass have caterpillar tracks attached to them to overcome friction and to make them more like mini-carts (or open-top tanks). Apart from that, the same rules apply: take the sledge to the top of a slope and push off. Applying the brakes will turn the sledge and of course bring it a stop! Grass sledges are available to buy but are very expensive; they can be hired cheaply from adventure companies.

## SLIDE... BY MUD-SLIDING

Fancy getting really dirty? Find a muddy hill (probably best after a few days of rain) and use a bin liner to slide down – you might not even need it if it's slippery enough! Wear some old clothes and take along a change of clothes.

# DO SWIM

Swimming outdoors is usually reserved for holidays in warm climes, but there's no reason why you can't 'dip your toe into the water' when closer to home.

Outdoor or wild swimming has to be one of the most invigorating adventure activities there is. Being out of your depth, in water you can't see to the bottom of, is quite a thrilling experience. The temperature of wild water (usually lower than expected or hoped) also adds an extra element of exhilaration.

A midweek wild swim with children, especially young ones, need not be anything too adventurous. In fact, the obvious dangers with this activity are heightened when children are involved, so always err on the side of caution and safety. The use of appropriate flotation devices is always advised, as is the wearing of a wetsuit (little ones are much more vulnerable to the cold than adults). Wearing light footwear is also a good idea.

When wild swimming, take plenty of warm clothes to change into after you swim.

Places to consider (in order of challenge):

### SWIM... IN THE SEA
All things considered, the sea is perhaps the most dangerous location in which to swim; there could be tides, current and waves. That said, swimming within the designated area on a beach with a lifeguard, in flat, calm conditions is relatively safe.

### SWIM... IN A TIDE POOL
Often only in existence at low tide, tide pools contain seawater that has been trapped by surrounding rocks. These shallow and safe, sandy-based tide pools can be fun places to float around in.

### BEAT THE CLOCK
Research and visit a suitable location for a wild swim in advance.

## SWIM... IN A LIDO

Outdoor swimming pools are a good first step for young or weak swimmers. There are usually facilities for changing (and getting warm) and there is often lifeguard cover. Importantly, the water will be clear enough to see the bottom and will gradually ramp from shallow to deep.

## SWIM... IN LAKES AND LOCHS

The gradual beach of a lake or loch can give safe access into the water, free from dangerous rocks or deep drops. Start by paddling then wade in a bit deeper until you are ready to submerge and swim in the shallows (where the water will be warmest).

# DO THROW YOURSELF INTO IT

Sometimes the more you put into something, the more you get out of it. This saying certainly applies to this activity – so, go on, throw yourself into it!

It is much better to throw things outdoors where there is more space (and fewer things to break). And when liberated by the lack of boundaries and constraints that being indoors brings, you can throw things harder, further and faster, developing the technique and muscles required for throwing long distances. An abundance of throwing materials (twigs, pebbles, seeds and nuts) means you have a supply of projectiles and can easily make targets to throw at (developing aim and accuracy).

Try some of the ideas listed below or make up some games of your own, but remember to be aware of other people so they don't get hit or hurt.

### THROW YOURSELF INTO... SPINNING SEED

Trees like sycamore cast off 'helicopter' seeds in the autumn – it's called seed dispersal. Use some seeds to have a throwing contest. Who can throw a seed the furthest, or the highest? Who can keep their seed in the air for the longest time?

Make a spinning seed to throw:
1. Cut a strip of paper.
2. Fold the strip in half.
3. Fold the tops of the paper over – one to the left and one to the right.

### THROW YOURSELF INTO... FLOUR-BALLING

Cut some old cotton fabric into small squares (10 x 10cm/4 x 4in) and place some flour in the middle. Gather up the material and trap the flour inside using an elastic band. Make lots of 'flour balls' and share them out. You are now ready to play your own version of paint-balling – except flour balls don't hurt when you get hit!

### BEAT THE CLOCK
Make the flour balls the night before you need them – it will save valuable time.

## THROW YOURSELF INTO...
## VARIATIONS OF GOLF

**THR-OLF** Take a ball out with you the next time you go to a forest or playing field. Choose something in the distance as your 'flag/hole'. Throw the ball towards the hole, counting how many throws it takes. The idea is to reach the hole in as few throws as possible. Make it a competitive game by having a ball for each person and keep score.

**DISC GOLF** Similar to thr-olf except you use a Frisbee. Some parks and open spaces have disc golf targets for you to throw at, but you don't really need them – just choose a tree or dustbin to aim at.

## THROW YOURSELF INTO...
## SEEDS AND NUTS

Seeds and nuts are natural ammunition for throwing at natural targets like tree trunks or hanging branches. If you happen to find any discarded drinks cans or bottles, stand them up on a log and then try and knock them over. You may not win a coconut, but you will be helping with seed dispersal. Put the bottles and cans in a bin before you leave and you'll also have helped to tidy the environment. Everyone's a winner!

# DO WALK

**These boots are made for walking and that's just what we'll do. Whether it's boots, trainers or wellies, it's good to get out for a walk with the family.**

Modern society involves an increased reliance on travelling by car and, in comparison to a few decades ago, children walk far less than previous generations. Walking does not only have to be a purposeful task of getting from A to B but also can be enjoyable, rewarding and fun. Walking in the dark, in silence, in rain, in sun or into the unknown can provide a different thrill to a normal walk within a known location so encourage youngsters to explore their surroundings like true adventurers. Don't let the weather stop you; just be prepared for it.

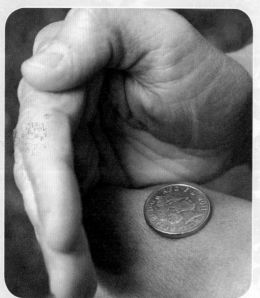

### WALK... INTO THE UNKNOWN
Rather than rely on a map or signage, use a coin to dictate the directions that you take. As you approach a junction, flip the coin to decide whether to turn left or right. Ideally do this in an area that you are familiar with, so that you don't get lost and can always return.

### WALK... IN SILENCE
Whatever the location, there are always sounds that we often miss as we talk or our minds drift to think about other things. Treat this walk as a 'listening' walk and purposefully listen to all the sounds around you.

### WALK... SOMEWHERE AND BACK
This may seem pretty obvious, but rather than taking an obvious route to 'somewhere' and back think about finding different alternative routes so that you don't need to retrace your steps. This might mean a longer journey but it might also allow you to stumble (not literally) upon an unknown area that you may have never seen before.

 **BEAT THE CLOCK**
For this activity you might need to look at some maps and work out different paths or routes that you could follow.

## WALK... AROUND A LAKE

There are some very picturesque walks around lakes that not only take in views of the water itself but also the surrounding woodland or hillsides. Some of these walks are well established and have signs but in some cases you may need to make your own path.

## WALK... IN THE DARK

A location feels very different at night. Go out onto the local streets, into the woods, along a beach or river that you might know well during the day and explore it in the dark with a torch. Alternatively, take a longer walk, e.g. climb up a hill at dusk and walk back in the dark, with the aid of a map, a torch and a compass.

# DO WATCH

**Rather than sit in front of the TV for a few hours, get outdoors and watch what is happening in the world.**

Many children in the modern world spend excessive amounts of time watching television or glued to a computer screen. While technology has its benefits, it needs to be balanced with the healthy outdoors. So for one night (or more), replace the screen and watch something together outdoors. You might choose to GO to some specific locations because of what you'll be able to see there as well as DO.

## WATCH... A SUNSET

Certain locations lend themselves beautifully to viewing the wonderful sight of a vivid sunset. Walking up a hill or finding a dramatic viewpoint will enhance the view of the horizon as you watch the sun slowly disappear, hopefully producing a spectrum of colours.

## WATCH... MIGRATING BIRDS

At certain times of the year, birds such as geese or swallows migrate to warmer or colder climates and watching them fly en masse is an impressive sight. Head to a lake, beach or nature reserve, taking along some binoculars, and watch the flocks of birds fill the air. The best time to go is early in the morning at dawn or at dusk, as the evening approaches. If you go to a nature reserve, particularly one that focuses on birds, experts should be able to give you information about the wildlife.

## WATCH... CLOUDS

You can be creative or scientific in your cloud watching. Clouds form different shapes and patterns that have specific meteorological names; you could learn some of these and try to spot them. Alternatively, you could lie on your back and stare at the clouds passing overhead, naming any interesting shapes (animals, characters etc.) that they form. This activity could also be done whilst walking.

## WATCH... A METEOR SHOWER

A meteor shower can make a spectacular show of lights in the sky. Choose a dark location with as little light pollution as possible and recline, looking up at the night sky, waiting for the show. Take along some binoculars or a telescope to get a better view if you can.

You might even consider camping (particularly in bivvy bags) so that you can appreciate the night sky 'show' later on.

## BEAT THE CLOCK

Rather than rely on pot luck, carry out some research and find out when there is going to be a meteor shower. Consider the time of year and weather conditions; taking a prepared bag that contains layers of clothing, snacks and drinks will keep everyone happy.

# DO WATCH AN EVENT

Watching an event may help stimulate a new interest or passion, but if not, it's still likely to be more exciting than watching TV or a computer screen.

Watching an event live with your own eyes can be an exciting and multi-sensory experience. Look for events in your local area, particularly around holiday times, but also keep an eye open for things that are happening at the weekends and midweek.

### WATCH AN EVENT...
### A FAIR OR A CIRCUS

Fairs and circuses are fun places for families, but are not cheap to attend. Enquire before you book and pay to go to a circus as to whether animals are used in the performance; this may influence your decision about whether to go or not.

### WATCH AN EVENT...
### OUTDOOR MUSIC

Look for outdoor concerts in forests and parks but also watch out for bands, orchestras or choirs performing in bandstands or other smaller venues where you can get up close. Listening to or watching buskers and street artists is also an enjoyable way to spend time in the outdoors. You never know, you may see the next up-and-coming-star-in-the-making.

### WATCH AN EVENT...
### A RACE OR A COMPETITION

By watching others participate in races or competitions you may develop an interest and motivation to participate. There's something in our human psyche that makes competition and challenge appealing. Look out for bike races, runs, car rallies and motocross, climbing and bouldering competitions. Look at websites of local clubs and organizations as they often promote smaller events that way.

### BEAT THE CLOCK

It can be time-consuming to look online or through local papers for things to do and watch, and before you know it, you'll have run out of time if you try and do it on the day. Get organized and do your preparation well in advance.

## WATCH AN EVENT...
### FIREWORK DISPLAY

Not just reserved for 5th November, Thanksgiving or New Year's Eve, firework displays can be seen at festivals or anniversary celebrations. Keep your eyes on the 'What's On' sections of local newspapers and magazines.

## WATCH AN EVENT...
### OUTDOOR THEATRE

Outdoor theatre is quite popular in the warmer months of the year, and again may be associated with a festival. Seeing theatre outdoors, especially in some kind of natural amphitheatre, always seems like a special occasion because the weather and environment add to the atmosphere.

EAT...

# EAT EATING OUT TOGETHER

Eating together as a family is one of those treasured moments of the day when everyone can relax, share stories and spend a concentrated amount of time together. In our modern, fast-paced society however, the time around the end of work/school and the rush to do other activities is becoming increasingly squeezed. The evening meal slot can become a time-pressured part of the day, with a focus purely on the act of eating, often separately and at pace, in order to be able to move on to the next activity. Like much of life, the eating part can all too easily blend into the everyday routine.

Families may eat out occasionally in pubs or restaurants, or order a takeaway in an effort to break the monotony of daily life or to provide a break from cooking. But another way to escape the rut and enjoy eating together is to head for the outdoors and make the meal part of a mini-evening family adventure. The act of 'eating out' takes on a new meaning: you benefit from the rewards of fresh air, stunning views and adventurous activities that are carried out together. If you haven't eaten 'out' before, or haven't done so for a while, why not give it a try?

## STREET FOOD STALLS

Stalls selling street food often appear at festivals and markets; increasingly they can be found on our streets too. They offer a wide range of food from around the world and their appeal is the speed and freshness of the food that is cooked before your eyes and eaten moments later. Consider trying some street food when planning an adventure in a town or city centre, or on your local street. Be adventurous and try something new!

## PICNIC

Picnics are a simple way to eat out and are appealing to families because of their flexibility – after all, you pack them yourself. They can be as complex or as simple as you wish and may be adapted to appeal to each and every family member. You often see picnics being eaten at a variety of locations: beaches, parks, woodland and castles, etc. They are a popular choice for a mini-evening adventure activity.

## TAKEAWAY FOOD

Most people enjoy the occasional takeaway whether it's Chinese, Thai or Fish and Chips. The meal is often collected from a shop or even delivered to the home, but one simple way to eat out as part of a mini-evening adventure is to take the takeaway meal with you to your location, or to buy it at the location that you choose to go to, e.g. fish and chips on the beach.

## CAMPFIRE

There's something magical about sitting around a campfire together. Although they are often associated with scouting or large events, smaller campfires can offer a secluded spot to cook on and sit around on colder evenings. As with barbecues, there are safety implications and supervision of children is essential. Campfires obviously require fuel therefore the location is important and it needs to have a supply of wood. You should also seek permission to light a fire; it is forbidden in many places.

## BARBECUE

Barbecues are a common summer pastime; when the weather gets hotter, the barbecues emerge from their hibernation in the back garden. Smaller, portable or disposable barbecues allow you to take your cooking to other locations and on your mini adventures. Take along burgers and kebabs that can be cooking on the barbecue while you appreciate the view at your chosen location or enjoy your chosen activity.

## GET THE KIDS INVOLVED

Eating in the outdoors does involve a bit of work beforehand, so make it a family effort and get everyone involved. The kids can help to prepare the ingredients by chopping up vegetables and supervise the mixing, turning, stirring etc. Older kids can take on the role of head chef and plan, prepare and cook the meal for everyone else, giving the adults a welcome breather!

The next few pages provide some recipes to try when out on a mini-evening adventure. They include some campfire and barbecue recipes as well as some tried and tested one-pot dishes. Enjoy.

## GAS STOVES

A gas stove is the main cooking implement for campers and ideal for taking out on a mini-evening adventure. It can pack up small and be tucked into a rucksack alongside the ingredients for a tasty one-pot dish. Quicker than a barbecue or campfire, gas stoves are a good option when cooking a warm meal in the outdoors.

## MAKE A 'TUCKSACK'

Create a rucksack that contains all the necessary equipment for cooking a family meal when out on a mini-evening adventure. The 'tucksack' can be kept in the back of the car or by the door, ready to use as and when needed. Just add the ingredients at the last minute. Here are a few essentials to keep in your tucksack:

- Gas stove
- Gas
- Lighter (matches/ flint and steel)
- Saucepan
- Plates
- Cutlery
- Bag/container to store any rubbish.

- Spare bags in which to put any dirty dishes and cutlery to carry home.
- Wet wipes (for hands and dirty dishes).

# (EAT) BARBECUE RECIPES

Barbecues don't have to be prepared in the back garden. When you venture further afield outdoors, take along a disposable or portable barbecue to your chosen location and get creative by cooking some tasty kebabs.

## KEBAB RECIPES

As a way of mixing and matching vegetables in a way that suit the tastes of each and everyone in the family, kebabs are a great idea. Encourage the kids to get involved in the different stages: preparing a marinade, chopping and threading the food onto sticks or skewers, as well as turning them regularly during the cooking process.

## Chicken and tomato kebabs
Serves 2

Slice the chicken breasts into long strips.

Mix the flour and cumin in a small plastic bag or bowl and add in the strips of chicken, to coat them with the mixture.

Thread one end of a chicken strip onto a kebab stick.

Thread a tomato onto the stick and then pierce the stick through the other end of the chicken.

Repeat with more chicken and tomato pieces.

Place the kebabs on the barbecue, turning them over regularly as the chicken starts to brown. Always make sure that the chicken is cooked, i.e. not pink, before eating.

- 2 chicken breasts, free-range
- Plain flour (handful)
- Cumin powder (½ tsp)
- 4 kebab sticks/skewers
- Vine-ripened tomatoes (about 12)

# Spicy tuna kebabs
**Serves 2**

Cut the tuna steaks into large chunks and place in a bowl.

Add the soy sauce and lemon juice and leave to marinate while you chop the vegetables.

Slice the corn on the cob and cut the pepper and mushrooms into large chunks.

Thread the fish and vegetables onto the kebab sticks in whichever order you wish.

Pop the kebabs on the barbecue and cook for about 10 minutes (depending on the size of your chunks).

- 2 tuna steaks
- 2 tbsp soy sauce
- 1 tbsp lemon juice
- 1 corn on the cob, sliced
- 1 red pepper, cut into chunks
- Button or chestnut mushrooms (5 or 6)
- 4 kebab sticks/skewers

# EAT  MEAT AND FISH RECIPES

## Chicken Ballantine
### Serves 4

**Who says cooking outdoors has to be simple or boring?**
**This is a dish that will impress at home as well as outdoors, in the open air.**

Slice the chicken in half (but not fully) and open it out.

Flatten the chicken between two sheets of cling film. Normally you'd use a rolling pin but if you haven't brought one with you, a clean stone will do the job perfectly!

Spoon some of the soft cheese into the centre of each chicken breast. Don't add too much, or it will ooze out during cooking.

Roll each of the chicken breasts into a sausage shape to enclose the cheese.

Wrap the chicken 'sausages' tightly in clingfilm, making sure to leave a lot of cling film at each end.

Twist the ends tightly and then tie the ends together to make a handle. (This will help when putting your chicken into boiling water and removing it.)

Poach the chicken in simmering water for about 15 minutes. Remove the chicken from the water.

Stir the stock cube in to the water and add the carrots and peppers. Boil until softened.

- 4 chicken breasts, free-range
- Cling film
- A 180g (6oz) tub of garlic cream cheese
- 1 vegetable stock cube
- 4 carrots, sliced
- 1 red pepper, sliced
- 2 x sachets microwaveable rice

Then add the rice and warm.

Remove the chicken from the cling film and slice into pieces. Serve with the vegetables and warm rice.

# Ginger beef stir fry
**Serves 4**

There's no need to get a Chinese takeaway when you can cook all the ingredients yourself in the open air – much tastier, healthier and more rewarding. The cooking smells will make any passers-by envious!

Heat 1 tbsp oil in a frying pan. Once hot, add the carrots and soften.

Add the beef, garlic and ginger and fry.

Then add the remaining vegetables.

Splash in a generous portion of soy sauce (to taste).

Try not to overcook the vegetables; they need a slight crunch. Once the ingredients are almost completely cooked, add in the noodles to warm and soften.

- 1 tbsp vegetable oil
- 3 or 4 carrots, thinly sliced
- Beef, thin strips (or Quorn alternative)
- Garlic (fresh or purée)
- Ginger (fresh or purée)
- A bunch of spring onions, chopped
- 1 red pepper, thinly sliced
- Sugar snaps (handful), chopped
- Baby corn (handful) chopped
- 2 tbsp soy sauce
- 400g (14oz) fresh noodles

# (EAT) MEAT AND FISH RECIPES

## Tasty Tacos
Serves 4

Tacos are a quick and easy meal to eat in the outdoors. You don't have to wait for a Tuesday to have tacos!

Heat the oil in the pan.

Fry the onions and garlic together until soft.

Next, add the mince and brown for about 5 minutes.

Add the peppers to soften.

Add the mushrooms and the tomatoes.

Stir in the paprika and simmer for about 10 minutes.

Spoon the mince mixture into the tacos and add toppings of your choice, e.g. grated cheese, sour cream and guacamole.

- 1 tbsp sunflower or vegetable oil
- 1 onion, chopped
- 1 clove garlic, peeled and chopped
- 500g (1lb) mince, or a Quorn alternative
- 1 red pepper, chopped
- 150g (5oz) mushrooms, chopped
- A 400g (14oz) tin of chopped tomatoes
- ½ tsp paprika
- 4–8 taco shells

TOPPING:
- A handful of grated cheddar cheese
- 1 tbsp sour cream
- 1 tbsp guacamole

# Kedgeree
## Serves 4

Kedgeree is sometimes eaten for breakfast so if you fancy heading out in the early hours for breakfast alfresco, here's a recipe to try. Alternatively, this makes a tasty, satisfying meal for fish and curry fans.

To begin with, boil the eggs for 10 minutes in a saucepan of water until they are hard-boiled. Remove them from the pan and leave to one side. (This could be done before leaving the house.)

Cut up the fish into small pieces and poach in boiling water until it begins to cook. (You could add a little white wine here if you wanted!)

Once the fish is almost cooked, add the chopped mangetout and rice.

Once the rice and mangetout have softened, add a teaspoon of curry powder (more if you wish).

- 6 eggs
- 3 or 4 smoked fish fillets, e.g. cod or haddock (sustainably caught)
- 200g (8oz) mangetout or sugar snap peas
- 2 packets microwaveable rice
- 1 tsp mild curry powder
- 300 ml (10fl oz) crème fraîche

Then stir in the crème fraîche.

Remove the shells from the hard-boiled eggs and cut into quarters.

Serve each portion of kedgeree with a few quarters of eggs.

# EAT PASTA AND EGG RECIPES

## Spaghetti Carbonara
### Serves 4

**Spaghetti Bolognese is always a popular family dish but this simple alternative is quick and easy to make in the outdoors.**

Heat the oil in a frying pan. Once hot, add the onion and soften.

Add the red pepper, carrots and fry.

Once the onion and pepper are softened, remove from the pan and put to one side.

Cook the spaghetti in boiling water, according to the packet instructions.

Once the spaghetti is cooked, drain the water.

Add the onion and pepper mixture to the pasta as well as the chopped ham.

Stir in the crème fraîche and warm.

Add the grated cheese and allow it to melt just before serving.

- 1 tbsp sunflower or vegetable oil
- 1 onion, chopped
- 3 or 4 carrots, thinly sliced
- 1 red pepper, thinly sliced
- Spaghetti
- Several slices of ham (or quorn/soya alternative), chopped
- 300ml (10fl oz) crème fraîche
- 250g (8oz) Parmesan cheese, grated

# Berber Omelette
**Serves 4**

Inspired by a trip to Morocco, omelettes were never the same again afterwards. This is a tasty light meal full of flavour and spice.

Heat some oil in a frying pan and fry the onion until soft.

Add the red pepper and soften as well.

Add the chopped tomatoes to make a basic tomato sauce and stir in the cumin powder. Feel free to add any other seasonings that you might have.

In a bowl, beat the eggs and milk.

Pour the egg mixture over the tomato sauce but do not mix. Allow the egg to set on top; it will form a layer above the sauce, mixing slightly.

Serve and eat with fresh bread.

- 1 tbsp sunflower or vegetable oil
- 1 onion, chopped
- 1 red pepper, chopped
- A 400g (14oz) tin of chopped tomatoes
- ½ tsp cumin powder
- 6 large free-range eggs
- 2 tbsp milk

# Gnocchi
**Serves 4**

A speedy little Italian for you and no, it's not a Ferrari – something much tastier!

Heat 2 tbsp of oil in a frying pan.

Add the gnocchi and fry until golden brown.

Next, add the onion and fry until soft and golden.

Add the mushrooms and fry them with the gnocchi and onion mixture.

Tip in the peas and tomatoes and heat gently before sprinking over the grated cheese, allowing to melt slightly before serving.

For any meat lovers, bacon can be added to the mixture too.

- 2 tbsp sunflower or vegetable oil or generous knob of butter
- 500g (1lb) packet of gnocchi, (use 2 packets for big appetites or 1 for smaller appetites)
- 1 large onion, chopped
- 200g (7oz) button mushrooms, sliced
- A 400g (14oz) tin of peas
- 200g (7oz) cherry tomatoes
- Grated Parmesan or mature cheddar cheese

# EAT  CAMPFIRE RECIPES

Everyone loves to roast marshmallows on a campfire, but why not widen the recipe repertoire and try a few other outdoor food treats as well?

## Campfire hot dogs

Remove the bark from the end of a freshly cut stick (such as hazel). This can be used to skewer your sausage and cook it in the fire. Another stick can be used as a skewer for cooking your bread.

Make your own packet bread dough well in advance. Follow the instructions for making the bread dough and leave to rise according to the packet. This could be done at home and brought along to the campfire.

Remove a handful of dough and roll it into a long sausage shape.

Twist the dough around your stick, making sure that the dough is not too thick.

Hold the stick over the hot embers of the fire and allow the dough to cook.

Once the dough starts to brown and harden it will slide off the stick. Voila, you have a ready-made hole for your sausage to fit into!

# S'mores

**S'mores (some more) are an American/Canadian treat that takes roasting marshmallows to the next level of yumminess!**

Push a couple of marshmallows onto a skewer and hold them over the hot embers of the fire until they soften (or burn) to your liking.

Sandwich the soft marshmallows between two biscuits and remove the skewer. The choice of biscuit is quite important. It needs not to crumble easily. The Americans and Canadians use Graham crackers or Oreo cookies. Alternatives might include Digestives. If you're not using chocolate Digestives, place a layer of chocolate (pieces/buttons) on to the biscuit before adding the marshmallows. Allow the marshmallows to cool slightly and melt the chocolate before eating.

# KEEPING SAFE IN THE OUTDOORS

Evening adventures are important for the mind, body and soul, but they shouldn't come at all costs. Equally, we shouldn't let health and safety dominate proceedings and spoil all our fun. More often than not, keeping safe means using your common sense, thinking ahead, and doing a bit of forward planning, then making sensible decisions (such as to call it a day and head home if something doesn't feel right).

The key health and safety considerations mentioned throughout this book have been compiled into relevant categories and are listed below. Have fun, and keep safe.

### BEACHES AND CLIFFS

- Cliffs can be dangerous so take care when on or below them.
- Keep an eye on inquisitive young ones around the edges of piers, jetties and sea walls.
- Gulls can be aggressive around children holding food so be aware.
- If sea birds are flying overhead, don't look up – you might get an eyeful.

### OUT AND ABOUT IN THE OUTDOORS, GENERALLY

- Get into the habit of carrying a first aid kit, and check it regularly to make sure it's up-to-date and well stocked.
- Be aware of any allergies a child may have that are triggered by any specific plants or insect bites/stings and take the necessary medications.
- Wear appropriate gear for the weather and the activity that you choose to do.
- Don't try and climb any walls or fences to gain access if the entrance to a place is locked up.
- Make sure little ones know not to run downhill… EVER.
- Isolated viewpoints offer quietness and tranquillity as well as great views, but take a map and compass to ensure you don't get lost.
- Make sure kids are aware of any dangers that might exist in their neighbourhood – road safety, stranger danger etc.
- Make sure little ones know how to use garden tools safely, and always supervise them.
- Woods and forests by their very nature have spiky, sticky-out bits that can scratch and puncture; therefore make little ones aware.
- Watch out during 'fungi season' that children don't mess with potentially dangerous mushrooms or toadstools.

## BUILT-UP PLACES

- Avoid areas littered with graffiti-tagging (ugly 'signatures' sprayed to mark territory) as these might not be desirable places to be, especially at night.
- Even after hours, urban centres and hubs can be busy places, so road-safety awareness definitely applies, especially to children.
- Cities and towns can have unruly elements, particularly at weekends.
- Gym equipment is usually built for adults or large children, so supervise small children to ensure they don't hurt themselves.
- Take a few minutes before you start to check your play area is free of dog mess (and any other potentially harmful objects).

## RIDING OR SKATING

- Hilly roads with lots of corners and long drops are a hazard.
- Regardless of what you ride, helmets and associated protective clothing/gear are a must.

## ON OR AROUND WATER

- Look out for signs warning of blue-green algae in the water – it can be toxic for children and dogs.
- Take care near steep banks.
- Be aware of tide times, particularly high tide.
- Make sure children are always supervised around water.
- Supervise young children carefully at all times when around water.
- Watch out for slippery banks along the edges of rivers and streams.
- Take extra care around canal locks.
- Make sure children wear buoyancy aids at the water's edge or out on the water.

## ON HILLS AND MOUNTAINS

- Always let someone know where you are going and how long you are likely to be.
- Wear appropriate walking boots always and take wet weather gear too as a precaution.
- Take plenty of snacks and water with you.
- Make sure little ones know not to run downhill.
- Stick to a proven route and don't be tempted to go 'off-piste'.

# INDEX

A big thank you to all those people that we've met along the way who have supported and encouraged us.

## PHOTO AND ILLUSTRATION CREDITS

**PHOTOGRAPHS** © Tim Meek, with the following exceptions:

**Front cover images** TOP LEFT © Gregory Johnston/Shutterstock TOP RIGHT © TAGSTOCK1/Shutterstock MIDDLE RIGHT © Titipong Chumsung/Shutterstock BOTTOM RIGHT © Dave Willis BOTTOM LEFT © B Calkins/Shutterstock.

**Page background image texture** © Phanupong Ratta/Shutterstock

p4 © Gail Johnson/Shutterstock | p8–9 Galyna Andrushko/Shutterstock | p12 BOTTOM LEFT © Lapina/Shutterstock BOTTOM RIGHT © Marcel Jancovic/Shutterstock | p16 BOTTOM RIGHT © Martin Fowler/Shutterstock | p17 TOP © Jacek Chabraszewski/Shutterstock | p18 BOTTOM RIGHT © Ahturner/Shutterstock | p26 BOTTOM RIGHT © nico99/Shutterstock | p28 BOTTOM LEFT © Kostyuk Alexander/Shutterstock BOTTOM RIGHT © Andrew Fletcher/Shutterstock | p30 TOP RIGHT © pamuk/Shutterstock | p31 TOP © Air Images/Shutterstock | p34 TOP RIGHT © khssbob/Shutterstock BOTTOM RIGHT © Sue Burton PhotographyLtd/Shutterstock | p38 BOTTOM RIGHT © Chris G. Walker/Shutterstock | p40–41 © MNStudio/Shutterstock | p42 © taviphoto/Shutterstock | p53 © zlikovec/Shutterstock | p57 © YanLev/Shutterstock | p75 TOP RIGHT © Mark Krapels/Shutterstock MIDDLE IMAGE © David J. Fred/Four steps in tying en:Double constrictor knot (en:ABOK #1252) Creative Commons BOTTOM LEFT © sharky/Shutterstock BOTTOM RIGHT © Daniel Fung/Shutterstock | p79 © AG-PHOTOS/Shutterstock | p82 © Daniel Fung/Shutterstock | p83 © Alex Pfeiffer/Shutterstock | p87 © David White | p92 BOTTOM RIGHT © Tim Gainey/Alamy Stock Photo | p93 © Syda Productions/Shutterstock | p96 © BOTTOM LEFT © Versta/Shutterstock TOP RIGHT © VICUSCHKA/Shutterstock | p98 © Tanee/Shutterstock | p101 © Maslov Dmitry/Shutterstock | p105 © Dave Willis | p110–111 © Rawpixel/Shutterstock | p118 BOTTOM RIGHT © alexmisu/Shutterstock | p120 © BOTTOM RIGHT © Stepanek Photography/Shutterstock | p123 TOP © Arina P Habich/Shutterstock BOTTOM © Mikhail_Kayl/Shutterstock | p124 © eurobanks/Shutterstock | p125 TOP © Greenview/Shutterstock BOTTOM © David Pereiras/Shutterstock.

## ILLUSTRATIONS

**Front cover illustrations** © Podis/Shutterstock.